Pocket **BIOGRAPHIES**

Christopher Wren

JAMES CHAMBERS

SUTTON PUBLISHING

First published in the United Kingdom in 1998 by
Sutton Publishing Limited · Phoenix Mill
Thrupp · Stroud · Gloucestershire · GL5 2BU

British Library Cataloguing in Publication Data
A catalogue record for this book is available from the British
Library

ISBN 0 7509 1857 7

ALAN SUTTON™ and SUTTON™ are the
trade marks of Sutton Publishing Limited

Typeset in 13/18pt Perpetua.
Typesetting and origination by
Sutton Publishing Limited.
Printed in Great Britain by
The Guernsey Press Company Limited
Guernsey, Channel Islands.

Christopher Wren

Pocket **BIOGRAPHIES**

Series Editor C.S. Nicholls

Highly readable brief lives of those who have played a significant part in history, and whose contributions still influence contemporary culture.

CONTENTS

ACKNOWLEDGEMENTS

I would like to thank my wife Josephine for her patience and Andrew Lownie, Christine Nicholls, Jaqueline Mitchell and Sarah Bragginton for their assistance in the preparation of this text.

CHRONOLOGY

1632	**20 October.** Christopher Wren born at East Knoyle in Wiltshire.
1649	**September.** Wren is admitted as a gentleman scholar at Wadham College, Oxford.
1653	**June.** Wren is admitted as a fellow of All Souls College.
1657	Wren is appointed Professor of Astronomy at Gresham College in London.
1660	**28 November.** The Royal Society is founded.
1661	**May.** Wren is elected Savilian Professor of Astronomy at Oxford.
1662	**15 July.** The Royal Society is incorporated under a royal charter.
1663	Wren designs the Sheldonian Theatre in Oxford and the chapel for Pembroke College, Cambridge.
1665	**July.** Wren visits Paris.
1666	**19 September.** Wren is appointed to the commission for rebuilding London after the Great Fire.
1669	**19 March.** Wren is appointed Surveyor General.
1672	Work starts on St Stephen's, Walbrook.
1673	**14 November.** Wren is knighted.
1675	**18 June.** Work begins on the new St Paul's.

Chronology

1676   Work starts on the library at Trinity College, Cambridge.

1679   Nicholas Hawksmoor becomes a member of Wren's staff. Wren joins the council of the Hudson's Bay Company.

1681   **12 January.** Wren is elected as President of the Royal Society.

1682   Work starts at Chelsea Hospital.

1689   Work starts at Hampton Court and Kensington Palace.

1699   Work starts at Greenwich Hospital.

1708   **20 October.** St Paul's is completed.

1718   **26 April.** Wren is dismissed as Surveyor General.

1723   **23 February.** Wren dies in London.

ONE

A MIRACLE OF A YOUTH

In the summer of 1654, the famous diarist John Evelyn spent a few weeks at his old university, Oxford. At the end of his entry for 11 July he wrote, 'after dinner I visited that miracle of a youth Mr. Christopher Wren'.[1]

At the age of only twenty-one, Christopher Wren was already a fellow of All Souls College, but his reputation for scholarship and invention reached far beyond the university. If his contemporaries had been told that he would soon be a professor of astronomy and a founder of one of the world's great scientific societies, not one of them would have been surprised. But few if any would have believed it if they had been told that he was destined to be remembered as England's greatest architect. So far, the only evidence of the talent that would one day eclipse all others was the high quality of his technical drawings.

Christopher Wren came from an eminent clerical family. When he was born, on 20 October 1632, his father, the Revd Dr Christopher Wren, was one of the king's honorary chaplains and rector of the adjoining Wiltshire parishes of East Knoyle and Fonthill; his uncle, the Very Revd Dr Matthew Wren, a recent Vice-Chancellor of Cambridge University, was Dean of Windsor and Registrar of the Order of the Garter. Three years later, when Uncle Matthew became Bishop of Hereford, King Charles I kept his previous offices in the family and selected Christopher's father to succeed him as dean and registrar.

Young Christopher's early life at Windsor was serene and glamorous. He was the pampered only son amid five sisters in a prosperous, privileged and close-knit family. His mother Mary, who was the daughter of the squire at Fonthill, had brought a large dowry to her marriage and, in addition to his stipend as dean, his father had incomes from the parishes of East Knoyle and Fonthill, where he was still the rector, and from the much richer parish of Great Haseley in Oxfordshire, which the king gave to him in 1638. As Registrar of the Order of the Garter Dr Wren was acquainted with the most distinguished men in the kingdom. As Dean of

Windsor he was a respected member of what was then the most cultured court in Europe. When Christopher was not studying with his private tutor, his playfellows were noblemen and sometimes even princes. When the king's nephew, the Elector Palatine, came to Windsor, he and his chaplain, Dr John Wilkins, were lodged at the deanery. But it was not to last. Within six years England was divided by civil war, and the fortunes of the Wren family faded with the king's.

In January 1641, at the age of only eight, Christopher was sent to board at Westminster School, which was then unquestionably the best in the country. Across the road, barely two hundred yards away in the Palace of Westminster, a new Puritan Parliament was busy curtailing the authority of the king. King Charles I had managed to rule without a Parliament for eleven years but a disastrous war with his Presbyterian Scottish subjects had emptied his treasury. At the end of the previous year he had been forced to summon a new Parliament in order to raise taxes and pay the invading Scots to leave England.

In return for a promise of very little, the members of the House of Commons exacted a high price.

They passed an act prohibiting the dissolution of Parliament without its consent. They arrested the Earl of Strafford, who had commanded the king's army, and they arrested the Archbishop of Canterbury, whose high-church intolerance had been responsible for the war. On 30 December they arrested one of the archbishop's leading supporters, Matthew Wren, who had by then been promoted to the important see of Ely. Uncle Matthew was imprisoned without trial in the Tower of London, where he remained for the next eighteen years. Five days later the king led a band of armed men into the House of Commons and unsuccessfully attempted to arrest its five leading members. In anticipation of a war that now seemed inevitable, the Dean of Windsor took all the jewelled insignia of the Order of the Garter, and all the small pieces of gold and silver from the Chapel of St George, and buried them in his garden.

For a short while the life of the dean's family continued undisturbed. At the end of the Christmas holidays Christopher returned to school, where he demonstrated his precocious but unassuming scholarship by writing letters and poems to his father in fluent Latin. In summer 1642 Christopher's favourite sister, Susan, announced her engagement to the Revd Dr William Holder, a brilliant young mathematician, who had just given up teaching at Cambridge to become rector of Bletchingdon in Oxfordshire.

In the autumn, however, the storm clouds broke. At the end of October, after the indecisive first battle at Edgehill, a troop of Parliamentary horse arrived in Windsor under the command of an officer called Fogg, who claimed that he had a warrant from the king and demanded to be admitted to the treasury of the chapel. When the dean refused, his men broke down the doors with crowbars, removed all the gold and silver altar-plate and then looted the deanery. They took away the records of the Order of the Garter and many of the dean's personal possessions, including a harpsichord and two silver tankards which had been given to him by the Elector Palatine. The high-church, Royalist dean knew that this was only the beginning. London and the counties around it were so strongly in support of Parliament that he could expect to suffer similar treatment regularly if he remained in Windsor.

Christopher was safe enough. For all their dour severity the Puritans had not yet been brutal to any children. So far, their only interference in the affairs of the great schools had been an enactment which made it illegal to compel the pupils at Eton, Winchester and Westminster to wear surplices against their will. But for the rest of the family it was time to leave. As soon as Susan and William Holder were married, the dean closed up the deanery, assembled his wife, his son-in-law and all his daughters – their number now risen to seven – and set out for England's second city, Bristol, which had just been taken for the Royalists by the Elector Palatine's brother, Prince Rupert.

This was a bad move. Bristol was always under threat and it was soon under siege. The dean and his family had hardly settled in the city before they were trapped in it. Back in Westminster, Christopher was separated from them not only by distance but also by battlelines. When his mother died shortly after giving birth to yet another daughter, he was unable to attend the funeral.

On 11 September 1645, when all hope of relief had gone, Prince Rupert surrendered Bristol to Sir Thomas Fairfax. The Wrens returned to their old home in the parsonage at East Knoyle and soon afterwards learned that there had been another raid on the deanery in Windsor. Led by none other than

Cornelius Holland, the councillor of state whose charges of treason soon led to the execution of the king, a platoon of soldiers had dug up the garden and found the buried treasure. Three years later, when the Parliamentarians sold off some of their booty, Dean Wren managed to buy back his harpsichord and three precious volumes of the records of the Order of the Garter, but the altar-plate, the tankards and the buried jewels were never recovered.

East Knoyle was no more of a refuge than Bristol had been. Local Puritans denounced the dean for the 'papist' plasterwork and paintings with which he had decorated the ceiling of the parish church. The Wiltshire Committee deprived him of the living and, in the summer of 1646, when he was evicted from the parsonage, he took his daughters to live with the Holders in Bletchingdon, where he remained for the rest of his life. In the same year, Christopher left Westminster School. Travelling was easier by then: the king had been captured by the Scots and fighting had died down. For the next three years Christopher divided his time between Bletchingdon, where he was tutored in mathematics by his brother-in-law, and London, where he was the eager pupil of the famous surgeon and scientist Dr Charles Scarburgh.

There is no record of how the young Wren first became associated with Scarburgh. It may have been as a patient. The small and slightly built young man had been sickly as a child; and in 1647 he wrote to his father from London saying that he owed his recovery from a serious illness, and probably his life, to the care and expertise of this doctor. It may also be, however, that the dean and his son-in-law decided to take advantage of the great man's inactivity, after the Puritans had deprived him of his fellowship at Cambridge, and offered him their prodigy as a pupil. Whatever the cause, the effect was dynamic. Wren's years with Scarburgh were the years when his genius blossomed.

Scarburgh introduced his pupil to his friends and colleagues: two astronomers, Seth Ward and Lawrence Rooke; a mathematician, John Wallis; an anatomist, William Petty; Oliver Cromwell's physician, Dr Jonathan Goddard; an aristocratic Irish scientist called Robert Boyle and a man whom Wren had met before, the Elector Palatine's chaplain, John Wilkins. The Elector, who had chosen his chaplain more for his reputation as a mathematician than for his theology, was in London ostensibly to help negotiate a peace, and secretly in the hope that

Parliament might ask him to replace his uncle on the throne. Setting aside any religious or political differences, these scholars made up an informal 'invisible college', which met regularly to discuss science, sometimes in Goddard's lodgings, sometimes in a Cheapside tavern; and when he was in London, merry, modest, little Christopher Wren was one of the company.

Christopher Wren was not just Scarburgh's pupil. He was also his assistant and even his collaborator. He assisted in the preparation of anatomical experiments. He made pasteboard moving models of human arm and leg muscles which the doctor used in his lectures at Surgeons' Hall. When Scarburgh and Ward decided that it was essential to translate the revolutionary works of the great mathematician William Oughtred into Latin, a language that would make them available to scholars throughout Europe, they confidently assigned the task to sixteen-year-old Christopher Wren.

Beside his studies and other duties, Wren found time for an astonishing variety of projects of his own. At the age of only fifteen, he patented a device for writing with two pens at once and devised a deaf and dumb sign language using the hands and fingers.

He constructed a weather clock and several sun-dials, one of which reflected its image on to the ceiling. And he wrote a treatise on spherical trigon-ometry, which he engraved elegantly on a little brass disc for his tutor.

On 30 January 1649 King Charles I was beheaded outside the Banqueting House, the first purely Renaissance building in London, which Inigo Jones had completed for the king's father in 1622. By then Christopher Wren was more than ready to start studying for a degree, but there could not have been a worse time for a young man with such impeccable high-church, Royalist credentials – even one of such proven genius – to be looking for a place at a great university. His uncle's old university, Cambridge, which had served as the headquarters of Cromwell's New Model Army, was staunchly Parliamentarian and devoutly Puritan. His father's old university, Oxford, which had been the headquarters of the king, had been subjected to a recent purge. In the previous year the Chancellor, Lord Pembroke, had led a band of armed men from college to college evicting anyone with suspect beliefs or loyalties.

By a lucky chance, however, the enforced changes in personnel, which would have denied Wren

entrance to any of the other colleges, provided him
with an opportunity at one of them. After Dr John
Pitt was removed as Warden of Wadham, his office
was assigned by Parliament to none other than the
Revd Dr John Wilkins, until then chaplain to the
Elector Palatine.

In the early years of the Commonwealth the
liberal and pragmatic Dr Wilkins was the only head
of an Oxford college who accepted the sons of
known Royalists, including not only Christopher
Wren but also his cousins Matthew and Thomas,
whose father was still a prisoner in the Tower.
Perhaps he was the only one who could get away
with it: he had great charm and a strong instinct for
survival. Eight years after he arrived in Oxford he
married Oliver Cromwell's widowed sister Robina,
and a year later he was appointed Master of Trinity
College, Cambridge. With such a long and strong
Parliamentarian background, he was inevitably
removed from his mastership in 1660, after the
restoration of King Charles II, but within another
eight years he was so far restored to favour that he
was appointed Bishop of Chester.

More importantly, Wilkins had an insatiable
curiosity and was an eager supporter of all scientific

experiment and investigation. His faith in the potential of science was limitless. He believed that men would one day sail beneath the sea, fly through the air and walk on the moon. Although he had no practical talent himself, he recognized and valued it in others, and he recognized it in the young man whom he had first met in the deanery at Windsor. He welcomed Wren warmly to his college and gave him the same encouragement and assistance that he gave to the more experienced men who arrived there at the same time.

Cromwell and his Parliamentarians were not Philistines. They filled the empty posts at Oxford with the best men they could find. In the academic year of 1649–50, when Christopher Wren went up to the university, three members of the 'invisible college' joined him; Seth Ward to become Savilian Professor of Astronomy, John Wallis to become Savilian Professor of Geometry and Lawrence Rooke to become a tutor at Wadham. In the following year William Petty became Professor of Anatomy and Jonathan Goddard was appointed Warden of Merton. In the study of science at Oxford, it was the beginning of a golden age.

In the lodgings at Wadham which were then

occupied by the warden, there is a large bright room above the main gate with an oriel window. Wilkins assigned this to Ward and Wren and allowed them to use it as they pleased. Four years later they showed it to John Evelyn, who described it excitedly in his diary. By then it had long been known as the astronomy chamber and was crammed with thermometers, lenses, telescopes, magnifiers, models, a huge magnet and an instrument called a 'way wiser', which measured the length of a journey by counting the number of times the carriage wheel had turned. Almost all of them had been made by Wren or Ward. The only important exception was a model of a 'geometric flat floor', which John Wallis had designed to support the floor of an upper room where the length and breadth of it were greater than the span of any of the available timbers.

In the four years that filled the room, Wren rose from freshman to fellow. The university statutes were relaxed to enable him to take his BA degree in two years instead of four, and after another two years he was an MA and a fellow of All Souls. In the year that he took his BA he completed a tract on algebra, and while taking his MA he was assisting the anatomist Thomas Willis in his investigations of the human brain, providing him with impeccably accurate drawings of every stage of his dissections.

Under the influence of Scarburgh, Wren had added anatomy to his passions. In his early years at All Souls he made detailed measurements of all the components of a horse's eye and constructed a model of a human one. In 1656, in the presence of Wilkins and Robert Boyle, who had by then come to live in Oxford, he injected opium through a quill into the vein of a dog, inducing a temporary and harmless stupor, and he used a syringe to take blood from one dog and successfully inject it into another.

Christopher Wren was a pioneer of anaesthetics and blood transfusion but his greatest contributions to science were as a pure mathematician and what would now be called a physicist. He wrote four definitive tracts on the cycloid; and his experiments and demonstrations helped to define the laws of impact and paved the way for the work of others. When Sir Isaac Newton published his theory of gravitation in 1687, he acknowledged Wren's influence and paid tribute to Wren and Wallis as the greatest geometers of the age.

Wren loved science so much that he played with it. During his first eight years at Oxford, every great undertaking was matched by a dozen gadgets and fanciful theories. He built a large sundial for All Souls and presented John Evelyn with a piece of white marble which he had impregnated with red dye. Among many other things he made a talking organ, a transparent beehive, a hand-held compass, a loom that could weave several pairs of stockings at once and a variety of pumps and musical instruments. He wrote papers on new codes, submarine navigation, ways of making fresh water at sea, a cheap, quick method of embroidering bed linen, techniques for dredging and fortifying harbours and, significantly, the application of engineering principles to architecture in order to strengthen buildings. In the early years, the playful side of Wren's nature found an outlet in the timeless recreations of a student. He took part in plays and wrote verses, including a piece which was published in a satirical pamphlet, *News from the Dead*, as an introduction to a supposedly true story about a servant girl who had been hanged for murdering her illegitimate child and then revived by the group of medical students who had bought her body for dissection.

Inevitably, the shy and self-effacing young genius made more friends among the dons than the students. Nevertheless, the closest of the many lifelong friendships that he made at Oxford was with an undergraduate three years younger than himself, Robert Hooke.

Also educated at Westminster, Hooke started his adult life as an apprentice to the portrait painter Sir Peter Lely, but he turned out to be allergic to the smell of oil paint and in 1653 he went up to Oxford. Soon after his arrival he became a laboratory assistant to Thomas Willis and later helped Robert Boyle in the construction of the famous vacuum pump with which he formulated Boyle's Law – that the pressure of a gas is inversely proportionate to its volume. At the same time, he developed new astronomical instruments, devised improvements to the mechanisms of clocks and formulated a law of his own – that the extension of a spring is proportional to the force applied to it. It was Robert Hooke who introduced zero as the freezing point on the thermometer. He was also the first astronomer to observe stars in Orion's belt and the first botanist to describe the cellular structure of plants.

Hooke and Wren had everything in common. They had a passionate enthusiasm for all things scientific and mechanical. They loved the theatre. They shared a fondness for chess, claret and tobacco; and their addiction to coffee and coffee houses was legendary. The fashion for drinking coffee in England is said to have started in Oxford. The earliest known English coffee house opened there at The Angel, near the church of St Peter-in-the-East, in about 1650; and in 1655 a Royalist apothecary called Arthur Tillyard opened a second one close to All Souls. Christopher Wren and Robert Hooke were keen customers of both. Throughout their lives they met regularly in coffee houses, often several times a week. It was in these coffee houses of Oxford that they planned their projects and shared their discoveries; and it was to be in the coffee houses of London that they would one day plan the rebuilding of a city.

T W O

THE ROYAL SOCIETY

The most significant events in Christopher Wren's crowded career at Oxford, and perhaps the most significant events to take place within the life of the university in the entire seventeenth century, were the continued meetings of the group dubbed the 'invisible college' by Robert Boyle.

When most of the members moved to Oxford, the meetings were moved to Oxford as well. At first they were held in William Petty's lodgings above an apothecary's shop, where it was easy to obtain any of the chemicals that might be required for an experiment. But the number of members grew rapidly with the addition of such like-minded scholars as Thomas Willis and Robert Hooke. Petty's little rooms were soon too small for them all. By the end of 1650 the members were meeting weekly as the guests of John Wilkins in the spacious warden's lodgings at Wadham.

Now calling themselves the Philosophical Society of Oxford, the members began to exchange ideas with other European scholars. For Christian men of science it was an era of unprecedented freedom and energy. Before the Renaissance and the Reformation scientific principles had been as immovable and sacred as religious doctrines. Since then, throughout the sixteenth century, there had been several great pioneers, but the universities and churches had been slow to accept their discoveries. In 1530, when Copernicus proved that the sun and not the earth was the centre of the universe, his thesis was dismissed by many as heresy. A hundred years later, when Galileo agreed with him, he was imprisoned for it. By then, however, the academic and theological climate was changing; and by the middle of the century, the last vestiges of reactionary opposition had been worn down by reason. Wren and his contemporaries were the first generation to enjoy the full fruits of this long revolution. Most of them were deeply religious, many were in holy orders, but they now felt free to challenge and experiment, to explain the phenomena of nature by observation and deduction rather than by philosophical argument. They rejoiced as they discovered the diversity and potential of God's creation, and their joy was reflected in the tone of their communications.

In 1656 the French theologian and mathematician Blaise Pascal wrote to the Philosophical Society of Oxford under the pseudonym Jean de Montfort and offered to pay twenty pistoles to anyone who could solve two geometric problems. The first was to find, by analysis, the point of intersection of a given straight line with an ellipse; and the second was to find the dimension and centre of gravity of a body produced by the rotation of a cycloid. Christopher Wren wrote back with solutions to both problems, but in fact both solutions had been implicit in a more difficult problem which had been set over thirty years earlier by the German astronomer Kepler. At the end of his answers Wren teased his French interrogator by asking him to solve Kepler's problem, which either made it clear to Pascal that Wren knew where his questions had come from, or else mocked him for his ignorance. Unfortunately that was the end of the story. Although Pascal later corresponded with Wren under his real name about cycloids, and although he described Wren's answers to 'de Montfort's' questions as 'beautiful', he never came back with a solution to Kepler's problem – and he never paid the twenty pistoles.

By the end of the 1650s several members of the Philosophical Society had been appointed to professorships at Gresham College in London. The college had been established at the end of the previous century by Sir Thomas Gresham, the founder of the Royal Exchange, who wanted to make scholarship available to every adult citizen. Housed in his former home, a splendid mansion with a colonnaded courtyard in Broad Street, it had lecture rooms, a laboratory, an observatory and lodgings for seven bachelor professors of divinity, astronomy, geometry, music, law, physic and rhetoric.

Each professor was paid £50 a year and required to give one public lecture a week, in Latin in the morning and in English in the afternoon. Despite the variety of subjects, however, the college had begun to concentrate on science, and the qualifications of the professors were not always appropriate to their chairs. Once the physician Jonathan Goddard of Merton had been appointed to the chair of physic, it might have seemed that there was no place for another medical man, but when the chair of music became vacant the city aldermen, who made the appointments and often made up most of the audience, awarded it to the anatomist William Petty.

In 1657 Lawrence Rooke, who had gone to teach at Wadham when Wren went up as an under-graduate, was appointed Professor of Astronomy. After only a few months, however, he moved to the chair of geometry, and the aldermen chose Christopher Wren to replace him. At first Wren did not want to accept an obligation that would take him away from All Souls for at least three days in every week, but Wilkins persuaded him that for one so young the honour and the opportunity were too great to be declined.

So every Wednesday in term time, 25-year-old Professor Christopher Wren lectured an audience which for the most part was composed of men who were older than he was. Although his subjects were usually the astronomy of Galileo and Kepler, he never forgot the preoccupations of his commercial patrons and wherever possible emphasized the practical applications of astronomy to navigation. The only tinge of sadness in Wren's triumph was that his father had not lived to see it. He had died in the parsonage at Bletchingdon a few months before the appointment. In his last days he had entrusted his son with the precious records of the Order of the Garter and had made him promise to keep them safe and return them to their rightful owner as soon as there was a king again in England.

At the time, it seemed most likely that the next man to sit on the throne of England would be Oliver Cromwell rather than any heir to King Charles I. The revolutionary government was well established, even though its leaders were still arguing about a constitution. But by now Christopher Wren's reputation was also well established. His Royalist background was no longer a handicap, and his appointment at Gresham College had brought him his first contact with the rich and powerful worlds of the City and Westminster.

Through John Wilkins, who was by then married to Oliver Cromwell's sister, Wren was introduced to Cromwell's son-in-law John Claypole, who was a member of Parliament and Master of the Horse in the New Model Army. The affable Claypole was a keen amateur mathematician. Wren was soon a regular guest in his house. One afternoon, when he was dining there, his host's father-in-law arrived unexpectedly. As he often did, the Protector sat at the table in silence for a while. He had never met the famous young professor before but it was clear from his glance that he knew who he was. Eventually he leaned towards him and spoke. 'Your uncle has been long confined in the tower.'

'He has so, sir,' said Wren, 'but he bears his affliction with great patience and resignation.'

'He may come out if he will,' said Cromwell.

Wren was astonished. 'Will Your Highness . . . permit me to tell him this from your own mouth?'[1]

'Yes, you may,' said Cromwell.

As soon as the dinner was ended and he could leave without discourtesy, Wren said goodbye and made his way to the Tower of London, where he gave the good news to his imprisoned uncle. To his further astonishment, his uncle was not impressed. It was not the first time that he had received such news, and he was not prepared to accept his freedom on terms which required an acknowledgement of Cromwell's favour and 'an abject submission to his detestable tyranny'.

But the 'detestable tyranny' did not last much longer. Oliver Cromwell died on 3 September

1658. He was succeeded by his popular but incompetent son Richard, and England was soon on the verge of anarchy. While rival generals assembled supporters and prepared to fight each other to replace him, the best of them, George Monk, rallied enough good men to garrison London and summoned a free Parliament.

Gresham College ceased all academic activity and for over a year served as a crowded, insanitary cavalry barracks. The Philosophical Society, which had begun to meet there on Wednesdays and Thursdays after the lectures of Wren and Rooke, returned to Oxford, and in the absence of Wilkins, who had by then left Wadham to become Master of Trinity College, Cambridge, the meetings were held in the lodgings of Robert Boyle.

In May 1660, however, General Monk restored the monarchy and the exiled King Charles II returned to England. Amid the widespread rejoicing, no family was more joyful than the Wrens. The Bishop of Ely was released from the Tower of London and returned in triumph to his see. His son Matthew, who had been living in Oxford, was appointed secretary to the new Lord Chancellor, Lord Clarendon. The records of the Order of the

Garter were handed over to the new Dean of Windsor, and Christopher Wren went back to spending four days a week away from Oxford – two days travelling and two days at Gresham College.

In the same year, on 28 November, the first entry was written in a new journal. It recorded the names of the twelve members of the Philosophical Society who had on that day, 'according to the usual custom of most of them',[2] attended Wren's lecture at Gresham College. They included Boyle, Wilkins, Goddard, Petty, Rooke, Matthew Wren, the astronomer William Ball and the soldier and scholar Sir Robert Moray, who was now the king's chief adviser on Scotland. After the lecture they withdrew to Rooke's rooms, where they discussed the founding of a college for 'the promoting of Physico-Mathematical Experimental Learning'.

The college was to assemble on Wednesdays at three o'clock. In term time it would meet in Rooke's Gresham lodgings and in the vacations it would meet in Ball's chambers in the Temple. There was to be an annual subscription of ten shillings and a weekly entrance fee of one shilling. Wilkins was to be the chairman, Ball the treasurer; and a list of forty-one potential members was drawn up.

At the very next meeting, on the following Wednesday, Sir Robert Moray arrived with the news that the king had expressed an interest in the group and was prepared to grant it a royal charter. Immediately, the excited company began to write the first draft of a constitution. The purpose of the association was to remain the promotion of 'Experimental Learning'. It was to be independent and self-electing, and its membership was to be open to men of every religion and nationality. Known simply and confidently as the 'Royal Society', a name that was later suggested by none other than John Evelyn, it was eventually incorporated under its first royal charter on 15 July 1662.

The Royal Society was not the first scientific society in Europe. The Medicis had founded one in Florence ten years earlier. But it was soon the most influential and the most prolific, overshadowing the French Académie des Sciènces, which was founded by King Louis XIV four years later. For the rest of the century and beyond, its devoted members donated extravagant amounts of their precious time to its transactions. During the next two decades, when Christopher Wren could have justly claimed to be one of the busiest men in the kingdom, he sat on several of the society's committees and gave regular lectures to the members. In those years his demonstrations ranged from the dramatic use of gunpowder to raise heavy weights to the famous experiment with suspended balls, which proved the laws of collision and paved the way for the work of Isaac Newton; and throughout his life he returned doggedly again and again to his unsuccessful search for a way of determining longitude at sea.

While the Royal Society was being established, Wren resigned his chair at Gresham College and took on more responsibilities at Oxford. In May 1661, when his old friend Seth Ward was appointed Bishop of Exeter, Wren was elected to replace him as Savilian Professor of Astronomy. Later in the same year the universities of both Oxford and Cambridge honoured him with doctorates of civil law. At the age of twenty-eight, he was recognized as one of the leading men of science in the kingdom. As his friend Robert Hooke wrote, 'Since the time of Archimedes there scarce ever met in one man in so great a perfection, such a mechanical hand and so philosophical a mind.'[3]

Yet, despite all this early success and fame, Wren had lost none of his engaging modesty. When Isaac

Newton's tutor Isaac Barrow succeeded Rooke as Gresham professor of geometry in 1662, he praised Wren in his inaugural speech, saying, 'It was doubtful whether he was most to be commended for the divine felicity of his genius or the sweet humanity of his disposition.'[4] In the following year, when the French traveller Balthasar de Monconys visited Oxford, he made a point of going to All Souls to meet 'the Great Mathematician', whom he described as 'a slight little man, but at the same time one of the most civil and frank that I have met in England'.[5]

After taking his chair at Oxford, Wren continued to spend so much of each week in London that the vice-chancellor rebuked him for neglecting his duties. Apart from his frequent lectures to the incipient Royal Society, he was also attending the regular meetings of the committee which the society had set up to study the production of lenses.

Towards the end of 1661, when he was preparing experiments for the society on pendulums and solar eclipses, Sir Robert Moray came to him with orders from the king. His Majesty had seen some drawings of insects that Wren had made using a microscope, and he had heard that the young astronomer was building a large-scale model of the moon. Through Moray, he commanded that Wren should make a set of microscopic drawings for his library at Windsor and that he should build a royal copy of the moon model.

Wren agreed to make a copy of the model and at a private audience, his first meeting with the king, he delivered the beautiful globe with an inscription on its pedestal: 'To Charles II, King of Great Britain, France and Scotland, for the expansion of whose dominions since no one globe can suffice, Christopher Wren dedicates another in this lunar sphere.' But Wren did not agree to make the drawings of insects. Begging to be excused because the demands of his other work were too great, he managed to avoid the job without offending the king, and at the suggestion of John Wilkins the task was assigned to Robert Hooke instead. It was not the only royal order that Wren managed to avoid in 1661. He also turned down the chance to survey the port of Tangier and direct all the operations necessary to turn it into an effective fortified naval base.

In May 1662 the king was preparing for his marriage to the Portuguese princess, Catherine of

Braganza. As was customary, the dowry was already being handed over, and part of it was Tangier. The port had long been neglected. As it stood, it was of no use for a royal navy, and the merchant ships that chose to shelter there were easy prey for Barbary pirates. Through his cousin Matthew, secretary to the lord chancellor, Wren was invited to turn the port into a base from which the British navy could control the entrance to the Mediterranean. He was to be well paid for it, he was to be granted a royal dispensation to be away even more often than usual from his duties at Oxford, and furthermore it was indicated to him that if he took the job he could expect to be appointed Surveyor General of the Royal Works on the death of the present incumbent.

There was nothing out of the ordinary about this offer. By seventeenth-century standards Christopher Wren was an ideal man for the job. He was a mathematician who had specialized in geometry. He was an imaginative pioneer in the craft of engineering. He was an outstanding draftsman: he had even written about the fortification of harbours. At a time when there were no civil engineers, and when architects were either amateurs or else designers who had learned their craft through apprenticeship and experience, there could not have been anyone better qualified.

But the offer was hardly tempting to a newly appointed Oxford professor who was playing a leading role in the creation of the Royal Society. The pay was not enough to be an incentive on its own, the task was not enough to be a challenge and the expectation of becoming Surveyor General was almost meaningless. The present Surveyor General, a poet called Sir John Denham, was only forty-six years old and in the best of health.

Pleading that his feeble constitution would not be able to withstand a long period in the north African climate, Wren managed once again to refuse a royal order without offending the king. But the refusal was by no means a rejection of architecture. When his qualifications and abilities induced others to offer him an opportunity closer to home, he accepted it willingly.

Before 1661 was over the Bishop of London, Gilbert Sheldon, had commissioned Wren to report on the condition of St Paul's Cathedral and make recommendations for its restoration. Sheldon was a former warden of All Souls. He had been dismissed during the Parliamentary purge in 1648 but had returned briefly to the post in 1660, before being elevated to the see of London. He knew Wren and he knew he had all the qualities that were needed at the cathedral.

Like the harbour at Tangier, St Paul's was in a sorry state. It had been badly damaged by fire exactly a hundred years earlier, and in many places the fabric of the building was crumbling. Although the roof had been mended, the spire that had once dominated the London skyline had never been replaced. The only serious restoration work had been carried out during the reign of Charles I, when the great Inigo Jones had refaced the walls of the transept and built a classical portico at the entrance. During the Civil War, however, the Puritan Parliamentarians had taken down and sold off the internal scaffolding, with the result that parts of the roof had collapsed; and as Roundhead soldiers so often did with large and admirable buildings, they had used the nave as a cavalry barracks.

Great though it was, Wren's task was essentially a practical one, ideally suited to an engineer who had written a thesis on strengthening buildings. But in the following year, before he had started his report, he was offered two much more imaginative private commissions. The first came from his uncle, the Bishop of Ely, who asked him to build a new chapel at his old college in Cambridge, Pembroke. The second came from Sheldon, who was also Chancellor of Oxford. Sheldon asked Wren to build his university a theatre in which it could conduct its secular ceremonies, such as the conferring of degrees. In those days the ceremonies were held in the university church where the accompanying unbridled merriment often offended the sanctity of a consecrated building. Among the many reasons for the project, therefore, one of the least but one of the most attractive was that the generous and open-minded chancellor wanted to move the ceremonies to a secular theatre so that the merriment could be allowed to continue.

Wren accepted both commissions. At the time they could have been taken as little more than interesting sidelines in the career of a great academic scientist. But in reality they were the first steps in a change of direction. As his 'mechanical hand' and 'philosophic mind' became involved in the practicalities of the projects, his heart was won over by the craft. Chance had revealed another talent and fate was about to present it with an unimaginable opportunity.

THREE

FROM
ASTRONOMER TO
ARCHITECT

For Christopher Wren, and for every educated European gentleman in the mid-seventeenth century, the classical style of architecture, with its symmetry, simplicity and dignity, was the only appropriate style for an important building. Surprisingly, however, there was as yet very little true classical architecture in England. This was not because the English had been slow to appreciate the style. The simple cause, which had nothing to do with architecture, was the Act of Supremacy of 1534, by which Parliament had recognized King Henry VIII as supreme head of the English church.

In breaking with Rome, Protestant England had turned its back on Catholic Europe and had lost contact with the most important centres of contemporary culture. Before the Act of Supremacy, encouraged by the patronage of King Henry himself, England had begun to feel the influence of the flourishing Italian Renaissance. His father's tomb in Westminster Abbey had been sculpted by Torrigiano, and Italian craftsmen had arrived to decorate English houses. After the Act of Supremacy, however, the influence was only second-hand, clumsily interpreted from books or imported in a modified form from Protestant Germany, Holland and Flanders. The distorted proportions and confused classical motifs on Tudor and early Stuart buildings were always primitive and often pretentious.

The change did not come until 1616, when England's first real architect, Inigo Jones, returned from his tour of Italy clutching four heavily annotated volumes of the great treatise by Andrea Palladio. Palladio had been the first Renaissance architect to model his style on a true understanding of the ancient Roman principles; and Jones was the first to apply these principles correctly in England. But before Jones could spread his influence, the Civil War brought an end to all building. As a result, almost all the examples of classical architecture that Wren would have seen were the works of Inigo

Jones – the New Exchange in The Strand, the Queen's House at Greenwich, the Banqueting House in Whitehall, the Queen's Chapel in St James's Palace, St Paul's Church at Covent Garden, the Portico and other additions to St Paul's Cathedral and perhaps the lodgings built for Prince Charles in Newmarket. Beyond these, there were a few classically remodelled country houses, such as The Vine in Hampshire. There was a fine garden front at Wilton House in Wiltshire, which had been built for the Earl of Pembroke by Isaac de Caus under the direction of Inigo Jones; there were three or four houses that had been built by Jones's pupil John Webb; and there was the magnificent Coleshill in Berkshire, recently designed by an amateur architect, Roger Pratt. He had spent the Civil War inspecting the great buildings of Europe, in order, as he said, 'To avoid the storm and give myself some convenient education'.[1]

That was almost everything, the entire canon of pure classical architecture in England. The only other building worth looking at, and the only one outside the works of Jones that Wren is almost certain to have seen, was Newington House just south of Oxford. Newington, which is still standing, was sadly remodelled with a rectangular façade in the neo-classical style in the late eighteenth century. Originally it had a steep pitched roof with dormer windows and a cupola on the top. Based on a drawing by Rubens of the Pallavicini Palace in Genoa, it was the first Renaissance house to be begun in England after the Queen's House at Greenwich, and it had a profound influence on the tastes of a generation at Oxford. The builder, Walter Dunch, who was related to Pratt by marriage, was a professor of law at the university. In the early 1630s, just after the house had been completed, Pratt was studying law at Magdalen and the rector of the parish of Newington was none other than Gilbert Sheldon.

After the Restoration, Pratt designed a fine mansion in London for the new Lord Chancellor, Clarendon, which, like Coleshill, was an evolution of the design that had been introduced at Newington. At the same time another amateur, Hugh May, who had been living in exile with the king, began to build Eltham Lodge in Kent, which he based on the houses he had seen in Holland. But by the time Wren started work on his commissions for the two bishops, neither of these houses was even close to completion. Apart from the obvious influences of Jones and the little palace at Newington, most of the ideas for his first two buildings came from books.

The design for the chapel at Pembroke was simple and elegant with a hexagonal bell turret on a wide pedimented roof supported by Corinthian pilasters. The theatre at Oxford on the other hand was a much greater challenge, both technically and aesthetically. A model of the design was shown to the Royal Society in April 1663, and in the following year the building work began. Based on the design of the ancient theatre of Marcellus in Rome, which Wren had found in a book by the sixteenth-century Italian architect Sebastian Serlio, it was shaped like the letter D, with seats for the audience ranged around the curve facing the long straight stage.

The original Roman building had no roof. When the sun was high, the occupants were shaded by a simple canvas awning stretched across the top. Wren wanted to reproduce the effect of this with a flat painted ceiling representing sky and clouds, with allegorical figures and the canvas and cordage of the awning pulled to one side. But the internal dimensions of the theatre were 80 feet by 70 feet.

There were no trees in the known world capable of producing beams that were either strong enough to support such a space on their own or long enough to stretch from one side to the other. Not even Inigo Jones had managed to support a ceiling of that size without using arches, columns or piers. Nevertheless, Wren knew that he had the answer. It was John Wallis's model of a geometric flat floor, which he had first seen in the astronomy chamber at Wadham, and which now stood in the king's private museum. Wren simply turned the design upside down. Where Wallis had supported the surface as a floor, Wren suspended it as a ceiling from a system of roof-trusses.

The Sheldonian Theatre as it became known was an engineering triumph, and it still serves the purpose for which it was built. Aesthetically, however, the exterior of the building was not so successful. The roof, which has since been altered, followed the example of Newington with a balustrade, a steep slope and a cupola, but the dormer windows were incongruously rounded and looked like precarious afterthoughts. As for the attempts at Baroque walls, the proportions were simply wrong, the straight south front bore no relation to the curved parts and the classical motifs were clumsy.

Even a mind as great as Wren's could not be expected to master so large a subject at a first attempt. But a mind as great as Wren's *was* capable of assessing and acknowledging its own short-comings. While the Sheldonian was being built, he was clearly dissatisfied with his work. In 1664, after the newly appointed President of Trinity College, Oxford, invited him to design a block of rooms for students, he decided that the time had come to see some of the great buildings of Europe for himself.

In July 1665 Wren set out for Paris. He was armed with letters of introduction, including one to the British Ambassador, Henry Jermyn, Earl of St Albans, and he was accompanied by two friends. Edward Browne was the son of an eminent physician, and Henry Compton, sixth son of the late Earl of Northampton, had just taken holy orders and was, like the ambassador, to play a significant part in Wren's later career.

Through St Albans and others Wren met most of the leading French and Italian architects who were working in Paris. He met Le Vau and probably Mansart, and by lucky chance he met the great

Italian sculptor and architect Bernini, who had come to the French capital to advise on the designs for the palace at the Louvre. In Paris, Wren made regular visits to the huge building site at the Louvre, where the machinery, organization and teamwork left a lasting impression on him. He visited the great buildings of the city and all the châteaux in the countryside around it. He saw and learned how men like Mansart grouped large rectangular masses, and he inspected structures that he had never seen before – domes. He saw the dome on the College of Four Nations, which is now the Institut de France, the dome over the salon at the château of Raincy, the domes on the churches of the Sorbonne, Val de Grace, Sainte-Anne-la-Royale and Notre Dame de la Visitation.

In a letter written from Paris, Wren said that he was preparing to write his 'Observations on the Present State of Architecture, Arts and Manufacture in France'. Sadly, the work never appeared, but notes that may have been part of the preparations were published in 1750 by his grandson Stephen in a memoir called *Parentalia*. Although most of the notes deal with the history of architecture, there are some that reveal Wren's principles and the extent to which he had been influenced by French building methods. In Paris he had learned that architecture had a political significance: it could make people proud of their country. Like the Romans he still believed that the essence of the art was order but also, like the great masters of the French Baroque, he now believed that the rigid rules of the ancient architects could be developed and modified to fit the mood of a more enlightened age.

By lucky chance, Wren's visit to Paris coincided almost exactly with the period of the Great Plague in London. When he returned to the sad but recovering city in March 1666, he was invited to join the commission set up to supervise the restoration of St Paul's. The other commissioners, who included Roger Pratt and Hugh May, had already received a report from the Surveyor General, Sir John Denham, in which he and his advisers had recommended the demolition of the nave and what was left of the tower. In hasty response, Pratt had submitted a report which argued passionately against anything so drastic. The confused commission now turned to Wren, whose own report was long overdue.

Ignoring his obligations elsewhere, including

those at Oxford, where he was still at least nominally Professor of Astronomy, Wren devoted almost all his time to a report, which he submitted on 1 May. He recommended that the work begun by Inigo Jones should be completed. The nave and transepts, which Jones had refaced on the outside, should be refaced on the inside as well, with tall Corinthian pilasters supporting the shallow brick domes that would replace the medieval vaulting. At the crossing of the transepts, nave and choir, he proposed that the tower be kept in place while a huge new dome was built over the top of it. In the beautifully drawn plan that Wren submitted soon afterwards, he showed a superstructure rising to a height of 360 feet. It had a metalwork pineapple on top of a lantern, which in turn sat on the splendid dome. The design of the dome was a combination of Lemercier's design on the church of the Sorbonne with another illustration from Wren's book by Serlio – Bramante's design for St Peter's in Rome.

The commissioners considered the proposals on 27 August and after much heated debate agreed that an estimate should at least be prepared. After that, however, there was no need to take the matter further.

Early in the morning of the following Sunday, 2 September, a baker called Thomas Farrinor failed to put out the fire beneath the oven at his shop in Pudding Lane. The house caught alight and a strong east wind spread the drifting sparks to the thatched roof of the Star Inn on Fish Street Hill. From there they spread to a candlemaker's warehouse in Thames Street.

It had been a long dry summer. The tightly packed, thatched and timber-framed houses ignited easily as the flames danced among them to the rhythm of the gusting wind. By morning three hundred houses, the warehouses on the Embankment and the north end of London Bridge were all ablaze.

After failing to persuade the indecisive lord mayor to pull down the houses in the path of the flames, the diarist Samuel Pepys hurried down to Whitehall to warn the king that the city was in chaos. To his great credit, King Charles came back in person to organize teams of firefighters and reward them with bags of coins. But for a while yet his efforts were not enough to compete with the gusting wind. The leaping flames jumped over every open firebreak that was put in front of them.

On Monday morning John Evelyn looked out across the river from his house in Southwark and saw the whole city burning from Cheapside to the Thames. The hot yellow warehouses on the waterfront were darkening the river with clouds of smoke from their precious stores of oil, pitch and brandy. On Tuesday morning, when the Fleet Prison caught fire, the prisoners were released into the streets among the panicking citizens. Under the command of the Duke of York, the king's household cavalry and guards were deployed among the abandoned houses to prevent looting. Militias were summoned from Middlesex, Hertfordshire and Kent to join the bands of citizen firefighters.

By Tuesday afternoon St Paul's Cathedral, clad in vulnerable wooden scaffolding, was blazing beyond all hope of restoration. It was not until Wednesday afternoon, when the wind died down, that the flames lost their momentum and were at last checked by the dramatic gaps that the king and his teams had created by blowing up the houses in their path with gunpowder. Over four hundred acres along the Thames were in smoking ruins, from the Tower in the east to Lincoln's Inn Fields in the west. The fire had not purged the squalid slums where the plague that killed 80,000 people had started in the previous year. Instead it had swept through the commercial heart of the capital: 13,200 houses, 87 churches, the halls of 44 livery companies, the Royal Exchange and the Custom House had been completely destroyed. St Paul's and the Fleet Prison were burned beyond repair.

Commissioners were appointed immediately to assess the damage and make recommendations, but at a time when the coffers of the king and the city were already depleted by war with the Dutch, their task was formidable. Over 100,000 people were homeless. In a century where the annual income of the city was £12,000, when the king's extravagant expenditure on Jones's magnificent Banqueting House had only been £15,000, the total loss was estimated at almost £10,000,000. There were many who believed that London would never recover.

OUT OF
THE ASHES

On 11 September 1666, less than a week after the Great Fire had been brought under control, Christopher Wren submitted a plan to the king for a splendid new city. He was not the only man to rise to the challenge. Two days later John Evelyn submitted a plan. Within little more than another week, Robert Hooke and Sir William Petty had offered plans to the Common Council of the City and the Royal Society. Other plans were submitted by a cartographer, Richard Newcourt, and a soldier, Captain Valentine Knight.

Hooke, Petty and Newcourt proposed precise gridiron patterns, although Newcourt also planned to increase the size of the city and turn it into a vast rectangle. Part of Captain Knight's plan was to surround the city from the Fleet to Billingsgate with a huge canal 30 feet wide. One of the objectives of this was to provide revenue by imposing taxes on all goods brought across the canal, but the king was so furious at the presumption that he would be prepared to make a profit out of a calamity that he had the poor man arrested.

The best plans, by Wren and Evelyn, were surprisingly similar. Both created dramatic vistas by joining great landmarks with broad dignified avenues. Both had a large octagonal piazza in the middle of Fleet Street with avenues radiating from each corner, one of which ran up to St Paul's and divided either side of it. Both envisaged other elegant squares and piazzas at the intersections of the avenues. But where Evelyn created five squares and crescents along the river bank and moved the Royal Exchange to the largest square, at the north end of London Bridge, Wren kept the Royal Exchange in its old position, making it the main focal point of the entire city, and converted the whole river bank from the Tower to the Temple into one long, broad, practical quay, just like the ones he had seen and admired on the banks of the Seine in Paris.

In Wren's plan the River Fleet was to be dug out and turned into a canal with a width of 120 feet. The central avenues were to be 90 feet wide, the others 60 feet and the streets 30 feet. All the trades that used fires or made smells were to be relegated to beyond the city limits. To the west of the area covered by Wren's plan, beyond the limits reached by the flames, Inigo Jones had once hoped to build avenues with vistas and fine churches around the piazza at Covent Garden. If the two schemes had been realized, the widespread grandeur of the two joined together would have made London a match for any city for centuries. But, like Jones's, and like all the other plans submitted in 1666, Wren's plan came to nothing.

It would have been possible to rebuild the city on a new plan but the process of compulsory purchase and redistribution which would have had to take place first would have been unpopular and slow, and it would have undoubtedly been accompanied by a great deal of bitter litigation. There just was not the time for all that. There were over a hundred thousand people to be rehoused, many of them living in open fields; all the businesses in the city were out of action and likely to remain so until they had premises; and furthermore there was a war on.

On 19 September 1666 a Royal Proclamation announced that London was to be rebuilt with wider streets in brick and stone. Six commissioners were appointed. The king appointed Christopher Wren, Roger Pratt and Hugh May; and the city appointed its surveyor, Robert Hooke, its leading mason and its leading bricklayer. In the following year, the recommendations of the commissioners were incorporated by Parliament in the first Act for Rebuilding the City of London. Buildings were to be standardized: minimum heights and thicknesses were specified for floors and walls. A tax of one shilling was imposed on each 30-cwt chaldron of coal brought into the city, in order to pay for the rebuilding of the gaols and the conversion of the shallow, stinking River Fleet into a navigable canal.

The responsibility for supervising this work lay with the city's commissioners. May went back to his duties as assistant to the Surveyor General. Pratt, who was knighted soon afterwards, inherited a fortune, married a rich, pretty heiress and retired to his Norfolk estate to enjoy his good fortune. Wren returned to his long neglected duties at Oxford and accepted a few more private commissions. In 1667 he completed the north wing of the new Garden Quadrangle at Trinity College, Oxford, which he had agreed to do before he went to Paris.

Sir Christopher Wren at the age of
seventy-nine, painted by Sir Godfrey
Kneller shortly after the completion
of St Paul's Cathedral. (By courtesy of
the National Portrait Gallery, London)

Wren's first royal patron, King
Charles II, by John Michael Wright.
(By courtesy of the National Portrait
Gallery, London)

Wren's diagram of the sign language for the deaf and dumb which he devised when he was only fifteen, from *Parentalia*. (British Architectural Library, RIBA, London)

Wren's first secular building, the Sheldonian Theatre in Oxford, was an engineering *tour de force*, but, as this contemporary drawing (from *Oxonia Illustrata*, Oxford, 1675) shows, the new architect had not yet mastered the subtle harmonies of classical proportions.(Courtauld Institute)

Wren's sundial at All Soul's College, Oxford. (Thomas-Photos, Oxford)

Designed in the same year as the
Sheldonian Theatre, 1663, Wren's
first ecclesiastical building, the
chapel at Pembroke College,
Cambridge, is much simpler and
more elegant. (RCHME,
© Crown Copyright)

The library at Trinity College, Cambridge, with a Doric order on the lower
storey and an Ionic order above, is a deceptively simple masterpiece of
composition. (RCHME, © Crown Copyright)

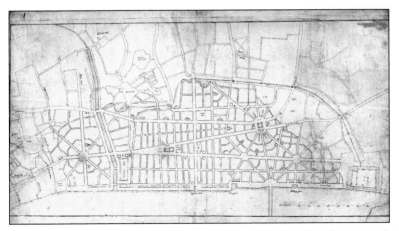

Inspired by Paris, Wren's plan of 1666 for the rebuilding of the City of London envisaged splendid vistas with long straight avenues connecting the piazzas and principal buildings. (The Warden and Fellows of All Soul's College, Oxford)

The first and most beautiful of Wren's towers and steeples, St Mary-le-Bow, contained the famous Bow Bells, which had survived the destruction of its medieval predecessor and continued to peal until broken by bombs in the Second World War. (RCHME, © Crown Copyright)

Like its medieval predecessor, St Paul's Cathedral looms over a teeming unplanned London. (*Illustrated London News*)

A cross-section shows the brick cone inside the lightweight dome of St Paul's Cathedral, which supports the weight of the stone lantern on top and is hidden by the false dome below. (Guildhall Library, Corporation of London)

Inside St Stephen Wallbrook, light, shade and the shapes of the masses and voids combine to create one of the great masterpieces of English architecture.(RCHME, © Crown Copyright)

Flamsteed House, in the background, which Wren designed for the first Astronomer Royal, survives amid later buildings at Greenwich Royal Observatory. (Greenwich Council Local History Library)

Wren's massive, Gothic Tom Tower dominates the medieval entrance to Christ Church, Oxford. (RCHME, © Crown Copyright)

At the request of his friend William Sancroft, Dean of St Paul's, he designed a chapel for Sancroft's old college, Emmanuel at Cambridge. The result is an unusual, pretty and slightly French building, in which the central chapel is joined on either side to the rest of the quadrangle by a long gallery supported on an open arcade. It is certainly the best bit of building in the college but the proportions are less than perfect, and the chapel's pediment and cupola are too heavy. It is still the work of the talented novice who built the Sheldonian Theatre rather than the genius who built St Paul's.

In 1668 Wren received a letter from one of his oldest friends, Seth Ward, who had just been made Bishop of Salisbury. His glorious cathedral was in a perilous state of disrepair, and he begged Wren to advise him. After a thorough inspection and a detailed report, all Wren's recommendations were carried out and the great building was saved. The roof vaulting, which he supported with iron braces specially made for him by naval anchorsmiths, is said today to be even stronger than it was originally when it was built in the thirteenth century.

It was while he was working on his report for Seth Ward that Wren received the urgent letter that was to set him on the course towards his greatest achievement. The letter came from William Sancroft, the Dean of St Paul's. At their last meeting Wren had whispered to Sancroft that the cathedral was damaged beyond repair: Sancroft could now report that the commissioners agreed with him. The king was about to order the demolition of the ruin so the time had come to plan a replacement, and the clergy were all agreed that nothing could happen without Wren. Fate was calling him back to London and, as if to make sure that he went, early in the following year, while he was secretly drawing the first of many plans, the king offered him a job.

Tall, stooping, pompous Sir John Denham had only been made Surveyor General as a reward for his loyalty during the king's exile. A poet rather than an architect, he was entirely the wrong man to be in that important office at a time when there was a capital city to rebuild. Quite apart from his questionable abilities, he was paranoid, unstable and much too preoccupied with his personal problems to pay more than cursory attention to his duties. In 1665, at the age of fifty, he had married an eighteen-year-old beauty, Margaret Brooke, who had almost immediately afterwards become the mistress of the

Duke of York. The eager lovers were so indiscreet that the affair was soon common gossip at court. As a result the wronged and humiliated husband suffered a bout of temporary insanity during which, among other things, he burst into the king's closet and informed the startled monarch that he was the Holy Ghost.

In January, 1667, however, the beautiful young Lady Denham died suddenly. Quite a few courtiers suggested that the Duchess of York had put poison in her chocolate but most people, including Samuel Pepys, said that the husband did it. Despite the fact that a post-mortem revealed no poison – and indeed no chocolate – the second story was widely believed. Hounded out of the court and jeered at in the streets, Denham locked himself up in his official residence in Scotland Yard, went mad again and eventually died in March 1669.

The time had come to choose a successor; and the job in hand demanded a good one. But in recent years the succession to the office of Surveyor General had not been a happy process. The last worthy incumbent had been Inigo Jones. After the Restoration, the best qualified and most deserving candidate to take his place had been his outstanding pupil and assistant John Webb. Indeed, Webb had been led to believe that the job would one day be his. But, to his outspokenly bitter disappointment, Webb had been passed over. Like so many offices after the Restoration, the job had been given to one of the members of the exiled court, in this case Sir John Denham, and Hugh May, a better architect, who had also accompanied the king in exile, had been appointed as one of his assistants.

Now almost sixty years old, John Webb expected that this time he would be appointed, but once again he was passed over. If it was not to be Webb, then the most obvious candidate was Hugh May, but May was also ignored. Within a fortnight of Denham's death, the king appointed Christopher Wren to the position. Webb was offered the deputy surveyorship but he turned it down. In a dignified but slightly scathing letter he said that he would have been prepared to serve jointly with Dr Wren but that he was not prepared to serve under him.

May, on the other hand, was as outspokenly furious as Webb had been after the appointment of Denham. Samuel Pepys recorded meeting him in the street four days after the appointment and feeling the brunt of his anger. Since May had just been promoted in the Office of Works to the role of Comptroller, the king increased his salary by a huge £300 a year; and in the following year he appointed him Inspector of French and English Gardeners at Whitehall, St James's and Hampton Court, which carried an additional salary of £200 a year. Clearly the king's conscience was not entirely easy about the way in which he was appointing surveyors general.

As Surveyor General, Christopher Wren was now in charge of the Office of Works. His deputy was the Comptroller, and the rest of his staff consisted of the teams which worked for the Paymaster and the Patent Artisans, such as the King's Master Carpenter and the Sergeant Plumber. His office was responsible for the care of all royal residences and all parts of London and Westminster that were royal property. It was also responsible for preparing royal apartments for ceremonies of state, balls and theatrical performances. But above all it was the role of the Surveyor and the Comptroller to design and construct new royal buildings. Wren's first major undertaking in his new role was to assist the city by designing a new Custom House. The result was a confident, imposing but still not quite balanced building, which, interestingly for the first project to be completed by the Office of Works under the new management, contained many elements of the Dutch style which May had used at Eltham.

At the age of thirty-seven, Christopher Wren was an established and powerful courtier, architect and academician. He had his own spacious official residence close to the royal palace and a salary of £316 a year, not as much as his Comptroller, but enough on which to run a household. On 7 December 1669, he was married in the Temple Church to 33-year-old Faith Coghill, the daughter of Sir Thomas Coghill of Bletchingdon, whom he had known since she was ten, ever since his family had moved there during the Civil War.

Very little is known about Wren's private life, and almost nothing about Faith Coghill. The only private document that survives from this period of his life is a letter that he wrote to her in the summer before their wedding. He was sending her a watch which had been mended after being dropped into a stream and, like every clumsy, fanciful lover, he told her that he envied it for being by her side and that he had put a spell on it so that every beating of the balance would be like the pulse of his heart, 'which labours as much to serve you and more truly than the watch'.[1] After he had signed the letter, however, the practical man of science got the better of him. 'P.S.,' he wrote. 'I have put the watch in a box that it might take no harm, and wrapped it about with a little leather, and that it might not jog, I was fain to fill up the corners with either a few shavings or waste paper.'

During his first months as Surveyor General, Wren still found time for the affairs of the Royal Society and for preparing experiments with his dear friend Robert Hooke. But in 1670 the second Act for the Rebuilding of London trebled the tax on coal. Out of the additional two shillings on each chaldron, one shilling and one-and-a-half pence were to be spent on the rebuilding of the city churches, and four-and-a-half pence was to be spent on St Paul's. The act also appointed three commissioners to oversee the work – the Bishop of London, the Lord Mayor of London and the Archbishop of Canterbury, who was now Gilbert Sheldon. But the real work was to be done by Christopher Wren and three assistants, the mason John Oliver, the surveyor Edward Woodroffe and Wren's friend Robert Hooke.

The great rebuilding programme had begun, and the huge demands of it were to bring Hooke and Wren even closer together. Over the next thirty years and more they dined together at least twice a week and met almost daily in a coffee house. Child's in St Paul's churchyard was inevitably the headquarters for the rebuilding of the cathedral, but Garaway's in Cornhill was Wren's favourite, although the refuge of Man's in Chancery Lane, beyond the boundary of the Great Fire's destruction, ran it a close second.

In the light of their achievements, it is hard to believe that either man ever had much time for anything other than work, but Hooke's diaries of those years give endearing glimpses of a life beyond architecture. They still found time for experiments, they visited their friends in the Royal Society, they held 'good discourse' late into the night, they made merry expeditions to the theatre and to fairs. One excited entry describes a trip to visit Robert Boyle, on which, 'near the coffee house at Bartholomew Fair', they saw an elephant 'wave colours, shoot a gun and carry a castle'.[2] There were times, however, when the entries were more laconic. In the entry for 14 November 1673, the day when the designer of St Paul's knelt before his king and received the touch of his sword on his shoulders, Hooke simply wrote, 'Dr. Wren knighted and gone to Oxford'.[3]

At the time Wren was making an unsuccessful attempt to get himself elected as member of parliament for Oxford, but perhaps the trip was also made out of conscience. Before the year was over Wren had reluctantly resigned as Professor of Astronomy, and for a while it looked as though he had accepted that even a man of his energy did not have time for everything. But his appetite for new horizons was too strong to be kept in check for long. Six years later he accepted a place on the council of the Hudson's Bay Company, and the records show that he attended regularly and that he often took the chair when the successive governors, Prince Rupert and the Duke of York, were not there.

The brilliant, depressive, self-effacing Robert Hooke had no domestic obligations: he never married, although he lived with a succession of young 'housekeepers'. But in the early years of the building programme Christopher Wren even found time for a brief family life which brought him equal measures of joy and sadness. His first child, Gilbert, who was born in 1672, died of convulsions after less than eighteen months. He had a second son, Christopher, in February 1675, but the joy was short-lived. Only seven months later his wife died of smallpox. Wren did not remain a widower for long, however. On 24 February 1677, he married Jane Fitzwilliam, the sister of the first Earl Fitzwilliam. It must have been a sudden match: in his diary entry for that day Hooke cannot even remember her name.

The second marriage was shorter and sadder than the first. Nine months after the wedding, the second Lady Wren gave birth to her husband's favourite child, Jane. But only seven months after that she gave birth again, this time to a tiny, mentally retarded son, William, and before the marriage was four years old, after a brief illness, she too was dead. William, who lived for almost sixty years, was looked after all his life by his father and half-brother. Wren did not marry again. The rest of his life, like most of the early part, was devoted to work and his friends.

The rebuilding programme replaced eighty-seven burned-out churches in the city with fifty-one new ones. On its own, it would have been a huge undertaking. But the programme was only one element in the rebirth of the city. By the time work started on the first church, 9,000 new houses had already been built. As years went by and churches rose, less spectacular building work was still going on around them. The city had not, as so many predicted, failed to recover; and the inevitably long-drawn-out revival was all the more remarkable because it coincided with war against the Dutch, Monmouth's rebellion, the Glorious Revolution and several of the hardest winters on record.

In addition, the two men most responsible for rebuilding the churches were involved in other building projects as well. As the City Surveyor, Robert Hooke was monitoring the reinstatement of public buildings and livery halls and at the same time designing and constructing Montague House, a new Bethlehem Hospital and a new Royal College of Physicians. As Surveyor General, Wren was designing new royal buildings, such as Chelsea Hospital. For most of the time he was also heavily preoccupied with St Paul's, where work began in 1675, and he was regularly engaged on private commissions, not only at the universities but also on two important new churches outside the city, both of which were to become models for dozens in the

American colonies. One was St Clement Danes in the Strand, which now has a tower by James Gibbs. The other was St James's on a large speculative development between Piccadilly and a new street called Jermyn Street, which was being financed by the ambassador Wren met in Paris, Henry Jermyn, Earl of St Albans.

It would have been quite impossible for one man or both to have designed all the churches in detail. Even after 1679, when the brilliant Nicholas Hawksmoor joined Wren's staff as his personal assistant, there was more work to be done than all three could have managed. They were a team supervising the activities of scores of others. Nevertheless, in looking at the churches, there are times when it is possible to discern the dominant influence. Sometimes the hand of Hooke can be seen, particularly at St Benet, Paul's Wharf, and St Edmund the King. Here and there Hawksmoor reveals himself in his masks, his idiosyncratic obelisks and his light-hearted Gothic towers, like the one on St Michael, Cornhill. More often than not, however, the evolving, harmonious genius of Wren is overwhelmingly obvious, particularly in some of the last to be finished, like St Stephen, Walbrook.

In many cases the decorations and details of the designs were left to the craftsmen of the parish, but as Hooke's diaries make abundantly clear, Christopher Wren was in charge. He was the director and the inspiration. The extent of his involvement in the decoration and design may have varied but it was Wren who created the plans for the churches, and it was Wren who came back at the end to crown them with their glorious towers and steeples.

Wren was building Protestant churches on what, for the most part, had once been Catholic sites. The shapes that he followed were the shapes of the Calvinist churches in Holland, which did not have choirs or transepts, but the models that he chose for these rectangular halls were the Roman basilica that he found in his books, and his interiors were much more splendid and elaborate than anything that would have met with Calvin's approval. The problem was that the sites of the medieval churches did not always suit his purpose. At the first two churches, St Bride and St Mary-le-Bow (which was based on Serlio's engraving of the basilica of Constantine) the large clear sites enabled him to erect rectangles with perfect classical proportions.

But on most other sites it was not so easy. Very few had any parallel sides of equal length, only a handful had right-angles at the corners and the Dutch-style church, St Benet, Paul's Wharf, which may have been by Hooke, was built on a steep slope.

The best of the best, and every inch of it by Wren, is St Stephen Walbrook. Even before it was built the parish was so pleased with the design that Wren was given twenty guineas in a silk purse. The exterior is simple and dignified but the interior is breathtaking. It has a nave and four aisles with a large central space, in which a dome is carried on a series of arches springing from eight Corinthian columns. The combinations of beautiful solid shapes make an immediate impact on all who enter; but as they move about in the sunlight and shadows, the changing shapes of the different voids become as dramatic as the masses.

In a few cases, usually where the walls had survived, the churches were rebuilt faithfully in the Gothic style, but at St Michael, Cornhill, St Mary, Aldermary, and St Dunstan-in-the-East, the whimsical towers owe more to the imaginations of Wren and Hawksmoor than to the Goths. Wren was particularly careful with the tall, delicate towers.

He played a leading part in designing almost all of them, he modified many of them several times and he took so long to get the designs right that they were often added long after the rest of their church was completed. To Wren they were much more than just finishing touches. They were the vital elements which brought the whole London skyline together in one composition. Some of them were still being built when the roof was being finished on the nave of St Paul's. But by the time the dome began to rise most of them were ready. The sky was scattered with towers, steeples, spires and lanterns, waiting like elegant fragile courtiers for the arrival of their king.

FIVE

ST PAUL'S
CATHEDRAL

While he was privately working on a plan for its replacement, Christopher Wren was given responsibility for demolishing what was left of old St Paul's and clearing the site. It was a formidable task. The huge ruin dominated the rubble-strewn waste every bit as much as the great cathedral had dominated the thriving city. The walls of the nave and part of the central steeple were still standing but the chunks of stonework that had fallen around them had been sealed into large solid masses by molten lead pouring from the vaulting. There was no option other than to break up the lead-sealed hunks laboriously with picks but the walls were in such a precarious condition that it would have been foolhardy for men to clamber over them and knock them down stone by stone in the usual way. Wren's solution was as imaginative as always.

He introduced a technique that has since become common practice for demolishing factory chimneys.

He used gunpowder. Wren had learned a bit about its capabilities when he conducted experiments in lifting weights with it, and with advice and assistance from the artillery officers at the Tower of London he put a charge under one of the angles of the steeple, which was still over 200 feet tall, lifted it a few inches with an explosion and caused the whole wall to collapse neatly on top of itself. Unfortunately, while Wren was elsewhere, attending to his many other duties, one of his assistants decided to repeat the procedure on another section of wall. Like a child with a recipe, he could not believe that a small amount of black powder would be enough and put in more than double the charge. The result was a much larger explosion. Pieces of cathedral went everywhere. One large piece ended up in the bedchamber of one of the few houses to survive the fire, and another just missed the head of a passing citizen.

After that it was no more gunpowder. Instead Wren reverted to more ancient military technology and used a battering ram. A 40-foot log tipped with iron was slung on ropes from a wooden frame. For a whole day thirty labourers swung it backwards and forwards against a wall. By sunset they were convinced that they had wasted their time but Wren insisted that the vibration would eventually be enough to have an effect. On the next day the stones beyond the battering ram's head slipped, the wall tumbled down and a new demolition procedure had been established.

The new design that Wren was preparing during the early stages of the demolition was surprisingly modest. It was a domed rectangle with long arcades on either side supporting the galleries which looked down into an interior very similar to that of St James's, Piccadilly. It was much smaller than any subsequent design, and it may well have been intended to be no more than a temporary structure designed to keep the dean and chapter in business until the funds had been collected for something better. But it soon became clear that the dean, the chapter, the entire clergy and the king were eager to have something much more substantial from the outset.

Wren went back to the drawing board. A domed Greek cross with concave sides grew on the paper from one drawing to the next. The nave became longer: a pedimented vestibule with a second dome was added. In September 1673, Wren showed Hooke the famous 18-foot model of it, which twelve carpenters had taken almost a year to build, at a cost of over £500. It was magnificent. Wren had abandoned the Calvinist shapes of northern Europe and returned to the traditions of Rome. The spirits of Leonardo, Bramante, Michelangelo, Mansart and Bernini had come together in a gigantic, palatial and Protestant rival for St Peter's.

In November Wren showed the model to the king: he was delighted. He approved the model, knighted the architect and set up a commission to rebuild the cathedral. But the king's approval and even Wren's friendship with the dean were not enough to sway the majority of the cathedral's clergy. The more conservative among them thought the design was too radical. The more worldly among them thought that it was impractical. They needed something that could be built in stages, so that they could begin to use it before it was finished and also pay for it in instalments as their share of the coal tax came in.

The design was rejected and Wren was heart-broken. Despite the splendour of his final achievement 'the Great Model Design' was always his favourite. In exasperation and fury he went through all his old designs, mixing and matching until he had cobbled together something that might comply with the prejudices of his clerical clients. On 14 March 1675, Wren left the Palace of Whitehall carrying a design with a royal warrant stitched to it. The warrant, signed by the king, gave orders that the building of the cathedral, in accordance with the attached design, was to start immediately. Soon afterwards Wren arrived with it at the cathedral's temporary chapter house. Fortunately, and as expected, the clergy liked the design and were happy to comply with the orders of the king. On 18 June the first contracts were signed and the work began.

The design, now known as 'the Warrant Design', was dreadful. It was a classical version of the traditional medieval cathedral, an old Gothic figure dressed in flashy Roman clothes with a tall Renaissance spire on top of an enormous dome. If it had been built, it would have looked from the distance like a Roman pagoda. But Christopher Wren never intended that it should be built. Nobody knows what passed between cunning King

Charles II and clever little Christopher Wren on 14 March 1675. All that seems certain is that the essence of what had happened was deception; and deception was to be the essence of the programme that followed, just as deception was to be the essential element in the design of the masterpiece that resulted.

There was a clause in the royal warrant that gave the architect 'the liberty in the prosecution of his work to make variations, rather ornamental than essential, as from time to time he should see proper'.[1] Wren exploited this clause to the full. The cathedral that he built bore no relation to the plan. 'From time to time', regularly, throughout thirty-five years, he put up what he wanted to build and passed off the change as an 'ornamental variation'. Yet from the outset there must have been a few astute men, apart from the king, Robert Hooke and the master builder, Thomas Strong, who realized what he was doing. From the very moment that the foundation stone was laid, when the ground plan was changed, the stonemasons at least must have begun to suspect that what they were about to do was not what they had been asked to do.

The dome was to be the dominant feature of the

cathedral, and the dominant feature of the London skyline. As a result, long before the building of the dome was begun, the need to support it influenced almost every aspect of the construction. The main support for the dome was to be a circle of eight arches resting on eight huge piers faced with Corinthian pilasters. But these alone were not going to be enough to hold its weight. In order to make it tall enough to be a landmark, and to enable it to be seen above the building by people who were standing close to it, Wren was going to have to set the dome on top of a large heavy drum; and in addition he wanted to crown it with a heavy stone lantern.

Again the answer was deception. Wren supported and strengthened the dome and the roof with medieval-style flying buttresses and then hid them behind a classical screen. As Inigo Jones had done at the Banqueting House, Wren designed the exterior of the cathedral to look as though it was two storeys high when in reality the interior was for the most part only one storey. This brought the exterior into line with all the classical rules of symmetry. But on the cathedral, unlike the Banqueting House, the deception was much more than just a matter of style and proportion. The substantial-looking upper part of the exterior wall had two further fundamental purposes, one aesthetic and the other structural. In the first place – aesthetically – it was the screen. There was no interior behind it at all. The balustrade, the pilasters and the imposing blank windows were simply there to hide the incongruous flying buttresses. In the second place – structurally – it was there to support the buttresses. The downward thrust of its weight at their bases strengthened them in exactly the same way as pinnacles strengthened the buttresses on medieval cathedrals.

When it came to the building of the dome itself, Wren borrowed a deception that had first been used by Michelangelo on St Peter's in Rome over a hundred years earlier. The problem was that a dome that was tall enough to soar over the city on the outside was also going to be frighteningly dispro-portionate on the inside. Standing beneath it would be like standing at the bottom of a large and very deep well. Michelangelo's answer had been to build an internal dome more proportionate to the interior of the building. Wren followed his example and built an internal brick dome inside the drum of the outer dome and then put a circular hole in the middle, through which light could fall from the crowning lantern.

This deception created more problems, however. And the answer to these problems was more deception. To be effective, the huge outer dome had to look imposing, but in reality it could not be too heavy because the drum and the inner dome would not be able to hold it. Wren's answer here was to build his 'heavy' outer dome out of Derbyshire lead on a light timber frame. But this in turn created another problem. The outer dome was not going to be nearly strong enough to support a large, Baroque, stone lantern.

Wren's ingenious solution to the last part of the puzzle has earned him the admiration of architects and engineers from all over the world ever since. Hidden inside, between the outer and the inner dome, he built a strong brick cone, rising from the base of the drum to support the lantern at the crest of the dome; and to prevent the cone from spreading under the weight of the lantern, he bound the base of it with a heavy iron chain. The result was the landmark that he wanted. The total height from the pavement to the cross on top of the lantern is 365 feet.

The interior of the dome was to be as sumptuous as the exterior was imposing. Above the famous whispering gallery the inner ceiling was decorated with scenes from the life of St Paul by Sir James Thornhill. One day, while Thornhill was working, he began to step back to admire what he had done and hovered for a second with one heel over the edge of his platform. Fearing that the great man was about to fall to his death on the marble floor over a hundred feet below, and realizing that a shout would be as likely to startle him as stop him, his quick-witted assistant smacked his paint-filled brush on to the piece of the dome that he was admiring. As he had hoped, his preoccupied master sprang forward in a fury, and his life was saved.

Wren was universally fortunate in the talent of the men who worked with him. Grinling Gibbons, who had been introduced to him by John Evelyn, carved most of the woodwork, including the casing for the organ, which was made by the German master Bernard Schmidt, known affectionately as 'Father Smith'. The iron gates for the north and south chancel aisles and the balustrading for the geometrical staircase were wrought by the French Hugenot emigré Jean Tijou, and among several fine sculptors, twenty-year-old Francis Bird carved the relief of the conversion of St Paul on the pediment over the main entrance.

It was at this main, western entrance that Wren had one of his few disappointments. Originally he wanted to support the pediment with a single range of gigantic pillars, but by the time he came to build them the huge stones that he needed were no longer available. A landslide had blocked the old harbour at the Portland quarry in Dorset, and it was no longer possible to load large stones into the ships that brought them round the coast to the Thames. After protracted negotiations with the notoriously querulous quarrymen, Wren gave up and compromised his design. The deception of his two storeys was reflected in two rows of much smaller columns arranged in pairs, with twelve pairs at ground level and eight above.

Wren was also fortunate in that he had a few influential friends in the clergy who were prepared to support him. Without them the cathedral might never have been finished. In the year when building started on St Paul's, and when the income of only £4,000 a year from the coal tax made progress painfully slow, Henry Compton, one of the old friends with whom Wren had travelled in France, was appointed Bishop of London. Compton wrote an eloquent pamphlet begging for private donations to help the building work and sent it to all the cities, universities and cathedrals in the kingdom. Soon afterwards, Gilbert Sheldon died and the Dean of St Paul's, William Sancroft, replaced him as Archbishop of Canterbury. As one of his first acts in his new office, Sancroft obtained an order in council which ruled that the tradition of giving gloves to guests at consecration dinners was to be halted and bishops were in future to give £50 to the St Paul's building fund instead.

To Wren's delight, Compton's pamphlet and the archbishop's order raised the available funds to between £10,000 and £14,000 a year for the next six years; and to his further delight he learned that the new dean was to be another old friend and a fellow of the Royal Society, Dr John Tillotson, and that one of the new canons was to be his brother-in-law, William Holder. His favourite sister was coming to live near him in one of the new houses at Amen Corner.

The next few years went well. Wren had his family and friends around him, and he had adequate funds for his projects. In 1677 he married Jane Fitzwilliam, and in 1681 he was elected President of the Royal Society. By 1684 the funds had begun to dwindle and the work was winding down again, but, paradoxically, on 6 February 1685, the financial future of the cathedral was briefly brightened by the sudden death of one of Wren's leading supporters, King Charles II. Like his father, the king had been ruling for a while without a Parliament but the new king, James II, was going to have to call one in order to raise some revenues. If Parliament was going to raise revenue for the king, it could raise one for St Paul's as well. Wren seized the opportunity and had himself elected as Tory member for Plympton St Maurice in Devon.

With Wren in the House of Commons and Compton and Sancroft in the House of Lords, it was not difficult to get the coal tax extended at one shilling and sixpence per chaldron until Michaelmas 1700, with the bulk of the income now going to St Paul's. But it was not long before it was far from easy to spend the money. The Catholic king was soon in open conflict with the established church, and the building work came to another halt.

Hopes were raised again by the Glorious

Revolution of 1688, which brought the Protestant William and Mary to the throne, but Wren was unable to join his friends in the rejoicing. Politically, he approved of the revolution but he was suspicious of the Whigs, who had engineered it, and privately he was still heartbroken by the recent death of his favourite sister. Susan Holder had just been buried in the crypt of the unfinished cathedral, where she was to be joined eight years later by her husband. As expected, the Whigs dominated the new Parliament and Wren lost his seat, but the new monarchs appreciated their Surveyor General and over-whelmed him with new commissions. Work began on the cathedral again, and for a few years the slow progress continued uninterrupted. But from 1696 onwards it was punctuated by a series of depressing setbacks.

The first of them came in February with the landslide at the Portland quarry. For several months there was no stone supply, and by the time it started up again there was no money left. Most of the stonemasons were still owed wages for the work they had done before the supply ran out. In 1697 the anxious commissioners estimated that it would cost over £178,000 to complete the fabric of the building, and they petitioned Parliament to continue the coal tax after 1700 for another sixteen years. After sending a deputation to inspect the cathedral, the Whig Parliament agreed, although it ruled that a smaller proportion of the income was to be spent on the cathedral; and in a high-handed attempt to make Wren speed up the project, it also ruled that he was to be put on half his salary until it was finished.

Christopher Wren bore this injustice with admirable dignity. On 2 December, when the king celebrated the end of his war against France with a service of thanksgiving in the newly completed choir, Wren must have watched with ironic satisfaction as the huge congregation, many of them members of Parliament, gazed around in wonder at what John Evelyn described as 'architecture without reproach'.[2] His only response to the insult came two years later when he sent in a bill for his expenses over the last twenty-five years and asked for £200.

The next setback happened on 27 February 1699 when the forge in which 'Father Smith' made organ pipes caught fire. Before it was brought under control, it had cracked and stained the masonry in the north choir aisle, and cracked the marble paving. It could have been much worse, but it still took two years to repair.

The new century opened with more setbacks on the horizon. The coal tax was producing only a third of what it had been producing before, and it was a bad moment for the building programme to be losing momentum. The cathedral was taking shape. Anyone with a long enough memory could see that it bore little relation to the plan. It was time to make one last push for taxes and reassure the citizens of London, who were paying them, that their money was being well spent.

As usual, Wren rose to the challenge. First of all he won over public opinion by anticipating yet another technique from a later century. He hired three of the best engravers, produced a series of prints showing views of the great cathedral as it would look when it was finished, and then made them available cheaply in the London print shops and distributed them free to all the leading politicians, churchmen and authors. As for increasing the coal tax, Wren guessed rightly that the imminent election was going to see a Tory revival. He stood and was elected for the constituency of Weymouth with Melcombe Regis.

He need not have bothered. King William died on 8 March 1702, and was succeeded by the high Tory Queen Anne, who was an admiring supporter of Wren and his work. Parliament was automatically dissolved but Wren saw no reason to stand again. Under the influence of the queen, the new Tory government was more than willing to support the cathedral. Although it took its time to make a decision, Parliament eventually raised the coal tax by as much as two shillings for eight years, more than enough to see the building finished.

Queen Anne celebrated her accession with a service of thanksgiving in the cathedral, and she returned to it several times for similar ceremonies. The most famous and most splendid was on 7 September 1704, when she walked down the aisle with the Duchess of Marlborough to give thanks for the Duke's astonishing victory at Blenheim. Four years later, in October, probably on the 20th, which was Wren's seventy-sixth birthday, a more simple ceremony took place outside the cathedral. The architect was hauled aloft in a basket on a tall crane to watch as his son Christopher, who had been born in the year when the building began, and the master mason Edward Strong, whose brother Thomas had helped to lay the foundation stone, laid the last stone on the lantern.

The years around the end of the building programme should have been glorious for Christopher Wren. He was famous. He was a hero at court. His masterpiece was completed and he was a favourite of the queen, who had made his cathedral central to the great ceremonies of state. But Christopher Wren was not happy. There was more melancholy than merriment in his demeanour. He was seen less often in the coffee houses. There was nobody to go with. His beloved daughter Jane had died in 1702 and had been buried in the crypt of the cathedral near her aunt. Robert Boyle had died long ago in 1691. Robert Hooke had died after a long illness in 1703. John Evelyn had died in 1706. The people who mattered most to him had gone, and he no longer had friends where he needed them. There was even a Whig in the deanery.

Towards the end of 1710 Wren began to ask for the half of his salary that had been withheld since 1696. The commissioners, particularly the new dean, Henry Godolphin, and the Duke of Marlborough's chaplain general, Francis Hare, attempted to stop the payment. In part they were incensed by the deceptive way in which the cathedral had been built and by the fact that Wren had not built it in stages as instructed, but there was also a degree of ill feeling over recent disagreements. They had argued acrimoniously over whether to have lead or copper on the dome, over whether to have wrought-iron or cast-iron railings, and on the style in which the interior of the dome was to be painted. At the request of the dean the commissioners had even dismissed Wren's master carpenter without telling him, on the grounds that he was stealing timber, and they would have prosecuted the poor man if the attorney general had not informed them that there was no case to answer.

When the queen and the Tory Parliament disregarded the objections and paid the arrears, Godolphin and Hare disgraced their profession and started a contemptible, underhand campaign to discredit Wren. An anonymous pamphlet appeared entitled *Frauds and Abuses at St. Paul's*, in which all sorts of charges were made against the craftsmen, and in which Wren, among other things, was accused of doctoring the estimates to his own advantage. Very soon afterwards an unknown friend published *Facts against Scandal*, which destroyed every point put up by the accusers. But sadly, and unnecessarily, Wren allowed himself to become involved as well. He was so angered by the attack on his workforce that, for the only time in his life, he lost his public dignity and published his own defence, together with a few bitter attacks on the commissioners and a detailed copy of his accounts.

The story of the creation of St Paul's Cathedral ended in a petty, discreditable anticlimax. The only fortunate part of the episode for Wren, who deserved none of it, was that he still had the queen and Parliament on his side when he asked for the arrears of his salary. They were allies that he was not to have for much longer. Queen Anne died in 1714. While the spiteful sniping continued, the Whigs looked round again for another monarch, and this time they turned to the house of Hanover.

SIX

THE ROYAL ARCHITECT

A s if the rebuilding of a cathedral and fifty-one churches was not enough, the fifty years that followed the great fire were also the years during which Christopher Wren served as Surveyor General to five successive monarchs.

Wren's first royal commission was to build an observatory at Greenwich for the first Astronomer Royal, John Flamsteed. There can never have been an architect better qualified for a job. Wren relished every moment of it. He balanced the octagonal observation room with little towers and turrets in a merry, romantic composition, which, by his own admission, he designed not only for practical purposes but also 'for the Observator's habitation, and a little for pomp'.[1]

The first large commission for King Charles himself did not come until 1683, when Wren started work on a new royal palace. It was to be in the ancient West Saxon capital, Winchester, close to the Solent, where the king could sail, and close to Portsmouth, where he could inspect his beloved navy. It was also to be a rival to the French king's palace at Versailles. Within two years, the palace was almost finished. The central part had a dome and a pediment on huge columns. On either side of the courtyard in front of it, two long blocks ran forward to two identical chapels, a Protestant one for the king and a Roman Catholic one for his Portuguese queen, Catherine of Braganza. From the sides of these, set further apart, two more blocks ran forward to the beginning of a ceremonial road leading down to Winchester cathedral.

But it was to be another of Wren's great disappointments. The king died, and his successors allowed the palace to fall into decay. After a while it was adapted and used as a barracks until 1894, when it was completely destroyed by fire. By the time the king died, however, Wren was well advanced on another royal commission, Chelsea Hospital; and at the same time, quite apart from all his ecclesiastical projects in the city, he had accepted two splendid private commissions at Oxford and Cambridge.

The Oxford commission, which came from the famously unpopular Dean of Christ Church, Dr Fell, was to build a tower over the main gate of his college. At first the Dean wanted the tower to double as an observatory, but Wren persuaded him that the tower would have to match the Gothic style which the founder, Cardinal Wolsey, had used on the rest of the quadrangle, and that an observatory could not have a Gothic roof. The result was the well-known Baroque-Gothic 'sugar-caster' which stands like a self-conscious heavyweight among the lean, bantam spires and domes in the Oxford skyline. It is one of Wren's few Gothic designs. It has none of the romantic delicacy that can be seen on Hawksmoor's designs at All Souls, or on the London church towers that they worked on together. But there is still a hint of Hawksmoor's influence. On 'Tom Tower' Wren played with his heavy Gothic shapes, grouping them and making them move, just as Hawksmoor played with heavy classical shapes on his churches.

The Cambridge commission was a small masterpiece. Sealing off the fourth side of Neville's Court at Trinity College, the library was designed to continue the arched arcading of the medieval buildings at ground level and light the interior with a long row of large matching windows above. Wren designed everything inside the library, even the stools, and for the first time, to decorate the panelling, he employed the woodcarver Grinling Gibbons, who had just been discovered by John Evelyn.

The Royal Hospital, Chelsea, was another of Wren's great masterpieces. Like the palace at Winchester, it was intended as a rival for a French model, in this case the Hôtel des Invalides in Paris, a home for retired and wounded soldiers, which Bruant had designed for King Louis XIV, and on which Mansart was now building a mighty dome. Using a similar design to the one he was using at Winchester, and also using the same materials, brick and Portland stone, Wren created a simple dignified building, which still serves the purpose for which it was intended, and which became the model for similar buildings for the next hundred years. In three storeys, with dormer windows above, it stands on three sides of a quadrangle facing the River Thames. The central block, which contains the hall and the chapel, has loggias on either side of a slim central portico with a tall cupola above it. Inside the wings, each veteran has, as he always did, a cubicle to himself.

King Charles II laid the foundation stone in February 1682, before work started at Winchester, but the project took much longer, and once again the king did not live to see it finished. This time, however, his successors kept the work going, and the hospital opened for service ten years later.

For King James II, Wren was employed on another unlucky palace project – an extension of Whitehall Palace, between the Banqueting House and the river, which was destroyed by fire in 1698. At the same time, while politics and the king's papist sympathies brought a temporary halt to most of Wren's other projects, he indulged in some profitable speculation. In partnership with a man called George Jackson he bought the site of burned-out Bridgewater House in the Barbican for £4,400, a considerable sum, and built a small estate of houses on it. Like many of the men who made fortunes in the wake of the Great Fire, the Earl of Bridgewater had originally intended to develop the site himself, and had hired Wren to design the houses. When he then failed to raise the funds, Wren joined up with Jackson, paid handsomely for the site and developed it himself.

The Glorious Revolution of 1688 brought

smaller but more fortunate commissions for palaces. King William of Orange suffered from asthma and did not like the low, damp, riverside air of Whitehall; and Queen Mary just liked building palaces. They decided therefore that they would live part of the time in the fresher country air at Hampton Court, and since the Tudor architecture was not splendid or classical enough for their tastes, they instructed Wren to extend it. For a London residence, they bought Nottingham House in open fields in Kensington and again instructed Wren to make it more palatial.

Building work at what was to become Kensington Palace started almost immediately, and Nicholas Hawksmoor was put in charge of it. But the impatient queen was so eager to move in that the work was rushed and the architects were never able to do as much with the house as they wanted. She came almost every day to inspect the progress, and the workmen cut corners to please her. As a result, in November 1689, a newly erected lead roof collapsed because the walls supporting it were too thin, and several men below were killed. Although the queen was duly contrite, the rush continued, and the royal family moved in for Christmas. Over the next few years, the 'improvements' went on around them with only one setback, one of the customary fires, during which the king and queen were seen standing in the dark on the lawn, roaring with laughter at the sight of the terrified ladies-in-waiting rushing backwards and forwards in their nightdresses.

During his first few months in residence at Kensington Palace, King William was preparing for his campaign in Ireland, where the exiled King James had landed a French army. It was this that gave rise to Wren's smallest and most unusual royal commission. He designed a small portable house, which could be carried in pieces with the army on two waggons and erected quickly when camp was made. Sadly, not even a drawing of it has survived.

The urgency at Kensington Palace was echoed at Hampton Court, only this time it was the king who was in a hurry, and the inevitable accident, only a month after the one at Kensington, brought Wren into conflict with his new Comptroller, William Talman, who was appointed to succeed the late Hugh May in 1689. For aesthetic reasons, Wren and the king disagreed as to how the flooring of the state apartments should be supported. The result was a compromise, and the result of the compromise was a collapse, in which two men were killed.

Wren and Talman submitted conflicting reports, and the inquiry that followed in Whitehall was entertainingly acrimonious. Wren described one of Talman's expert witnesses as a madman. Talman described one of Wren's as a liar. One of Wren's masons suggested that Talman's masons would not know good work if they saw it, and Talman himself questioned the competence of Wren's masons. In the end the inquiry never got to the bottom of what had happened.

The notoriously quarrelsome William Talman was a Whig. He had been appointed Comptroller on the recommendation of the first Duke of Devonshire who was a leader among the Whig magnates, who had engineered the Glorious Revolution, and was the patron for whom Talman later designed the south front at Chatsworth. There was very little other than a love of buildings that he and Wren had in common. Although Wren continued to work with him, he must have been relieved when Talman was dismissed on the accession of Queen Anne and replaced by John Vanbrugh.

The son of a Protestant refugee from Flanders,

Vanbrugh started his adult life as an officer in the Earl of Huntingdon's Regiment of Foot, but he resigned his commission when he discovered that he was about to be posted to tedious garrison duty in Guernsey. After that he went to France, where he was arrested in mysterious circumstances. When Louis XIV declared war on England in 1690, a Parisian woman denounced Vanbrugh for having left the city without an enemy alien's passport, and when French soldiers found him he was innocently making sketches of their fortifications. During the two years of imprisonment in the Bastille that followed Vanbrugh wrote a play, *The Provok'd Wife*. After his release, which was as mysterious as his arrest, Vanbrugh returned to England, served briefly but inactively in the marines and then took to writing plays full time. By the time of his appointment as Comptroller, he was a rich and successful playwright, second only to William Congreve.

Wren already knew him. In 1699, after quarrelling with Talman over costs, the Earl of Carlisle had instead invited his friend Vanbrugh to design Castle Howard, and Wren had tactfully suggested that, since Vanbrugh had never designed a house before, it might be useful to have Nicholas Hawksmoor as an assistant.

It was the beginning of a fruitful relationship. When they were not working with Wren, Vanbrugh and Hawksmoor designed several houses, including Blenheim Palace for the Duke of Marlborough. Those who admire them often give the credit to Vanbrugh, but even the briefest glance at the less impressive houses which Vanbrugh designed without the help of Hawksmoor will reveal just how much he owed on the others to the self-effacing genius of his assistant.

The scholarly Wren, the flamboyant Vanbrugh and the humble Hawksmoor were an incongruous trio but they were a good team. They worked well together. Like Hawksmoor, Vanbrugh admired and respected the Surveyor General. Although he was critical of the Office of Works, he was never critical of Wren.

Their great project was at Greenwich. In 1692, the sight of wounded sailors being brought home after the battle of La Hogue, inspired Queen Mary to build a naval version of Chelsea Hospital around the block that John Webb had built as the first part of a palace for King Charles II. It was to be a much more ambitious scheme than Chelsea Hospital, but the planning was inhibited by the queen's insistence that Inigo Jones's Queen's House should still be seen from the river. For all its beauty, the Queen's House was so small by comparison with what was intended that it was in danger of being dwarfed. Wren compromised by laying out the hospital in a picturesque composition of blocks with the Queen's House at the end of a long colonnaded vista between them.

Wren started enthusiastically on the project, with only Hawksmoor working as his assistant, but as time passed and age got the better of him, he involved himself less and less, until, in 1702, Vanbrugh took over the management. The block known as Queen Anne's block, facing Webb's building, was completed by Hawksmoor in 1715, and the façade of the west front was completed by Vanbrugh in 1726.

The accession of George I, in 1715, brought in a new dynasty, a new Whig ascendancy and a new distribution of jobs for friends. Hawksmoor and Vanbrugh were safe enough. Hawksmoor was inoffensive and his offices were too humble to be envied. Vanbrugh had too many powerful friends.

But tired, old Sir Christopher Wren was vulnerable. He had few friends left at court, none in Parliament and certainly none in the deanery of St Paul's. On 26 April 1718, King George I dismissed him and replaced him with his friend William Benson, a Whig gentleman with very little discernible talent. To add to the humiliation, Benson presumed to write a report criticizing the way the Office of Works had been run and questioning the probity of the previous surveyor. On 21 April 1719, almost exactly a year after his dismissal, Wren felt compelled to write to the lords of the Treasury, protesting that after a long life in royal service, and after having made some figure in the world, he ought to be allowed to die in peace. In the circumstances it can have been little consolation to him that Benson was dismissed in the following year for incompetence.

Wren retired to the house that he leased near Hampton Court, where he returned to the study of astronomy and wrote a memorandum in code on possible ways of determining longitude at sea. From time to time he came up to London and stayed at a house which he rented in St James's, and once a year he went to St Paul's and sat in silence under his dome. It was after one such visit, on 25 February 1723, that he went back to the house in St James's suffering from a chill. Later that day, after dinner, he fell asleep in his chair and died.

When historians draw up lists of the four or five greatest Englishmen, Wren's is one of only two names that always appear. It is perhaps surprising that an architect should feature in such a list, particularly an English list, but Wren was much more than an architect, and even as an architect his legacy was unique. In England, Wren was to architecture what Shakespeare was to literature.

Wren's life was so long that, unlike most of the architects who designed cathedrals, he was still alive to see his masterpiece when it was finished, and it was a masterpiece that took even longer than most. He saw his dearest dead laid to rest in it — his favourite child and his favourite sister. And when the time came he was laid to rest in it himself. He had asked in his will that he be buried without pomp but his funeral was far from what he wanted. The crowd of mourners and a score of coaches revealed that he still had more friends than he knew. Nevertheless he would have been pleased by his simple stone tomb in the crypt. Above it his son Christopher placed a small marble tablet engraved with a Latin epitaph, which reads in translation, 'Below is laid the builder of this Church and City, Christopher Wren, who lived more than ninety years not for himself but for the public good. Reader, if you need a monument, look around.'

LECTOR, SI MONUMENTUM REQUIRIS, CIRCUMSPICE.

A P P E N D I X

CITY OF LONDON CHURCHES DESIGNED AND BUILT UNDER
THE DIRECTION OF SIR CHRISTOPHER WREN

Churches still standing

St Andrew Holborn. Destroyed by bombs 1941, rebuilt 1960.

St Andrew by the Wardrobe. Destroyed by bombs 1940, rebuilt 1959.

St Anne and St Agnes, Gresham Street. Damaged by bombs 1940, rebuilt 1963.

St Benet, Paul's Wharf.

St Bride's, Fleet Street.

St Clement, Eastcheap. Badly damaged by bombs in 1940.

St Edmund the King, Lombard Street. Damaged by bombs 1917.

St James Garlickhithe. Hit in 1940 by a 500-lb bomb which did not explode.

St Lawrence Jewry.

St Magnus the Martyr.

St Margaret Lothbury.

St Margaret Pattens.

St Martin within Ludgate.

St Mary Abchurch.

St Mary Aldermanbury. Interior destroyed by bombs, but church rebuilt in Fulton, USA.

St Mary Aldermary. Damaged by bombs 1940 but restored.

St Mary at Hill.

St Mary-le-Bow. Bombed 1940, restored 1956.

St Michael, Cornhill.

St Michael, Paternoster Royal. Bombed 1944, restored 1967.

St Nicholas, Cole Abbey. Bombed 1941, restored 1962.

St Peter, Cornhill.

St Stephen, Walbrook.

St Vedast, Foster Lane. Bombed 1941, restored 1960.

Churches demolished when parishes were amalgamated under the Union of Benefices Act

All Hallows the Great, Upper Thames Street. Demolished in 1893 except for tower, which was destroyed by bombs in 1939.

St Dionis Backchurch, Lime Street. Demolished 1878.

St Matthew, Friday Street. Demolished 1881.

St Michael, Queenhithe. Demolished 1876.

St Michael, Wood Street. Demolished 1894.

St Mildred, Poultry. Demolished 1872.

St Olave, Old Jewry. Demolished 1888; tower still standing.

Churches demolished for other reasons

All Hallows, Broad Street. Site sold for development 1876.

All Hallows, Lombard Street. Demolished 1938 to make way for Barclays Bank.

St Antholin, Watling Street. Demolished 1875.

St Bartholomew by the Exchange. Demolished 1840 to make way for new Royal Exchange.

St Benet, Gracechurch Street. Demolished 1867.

St Benet Fink. Demolished 1842 to make way for new Royal Exchange.

St Christopher-le-Stocks. Demolished 1781.

St George, Botolph Lane. Demolished as unsafe 1902.

St Mary Magdalen, Knightrider Street. Demolished after a fire 1887.

St Mary Somerset. Demolished except for tower 1871.

St Mary, Woolnoth. Wren's restored church was pulled down in 1711 and rebuilt by Nicholas Hawksmoor.

St Michael, Bassishaw. Demolished as unsafe 1899.

St Michael, Crooked Lane. Demolished to make way for King William Street 1831.

Churches destroyed by bombs

Christ Church, Newgate Street. Bombed 1940, steeple, tower and vestry restored.

St Alban, Wood Street. Bombed 1940, tower still standing.

St Augustin, Watling Street. Bombed 1940, tower still standing.

St Dunstan in the East. Bombed 1940, tower restored.

St Mildred, Bread Street. Bombed 1941.

St Stephen, Coleman Street. Bombed 1940.

St Swithin, London Stone. Interior destroyed by bombs 1941.

NOTES

CHAPTER ONE

1. *The Diary of John Evelyn, 1637–1706*, ed. E.S. de Beer. Oxford University Press, Oxford, 1955, vol. III, p. 106, entry for 11 July 1654.

CHAPTER TWO

1. Christopher Wren (II), *Parentalia, Memoirs of the Family of the Wrens*, published by his son Stephen Wren in 1750. Facsimile copy in the possession of the RIBA reprinted by Gregg Press, Farnborough, 1965, pp. 33–4.
2. *First Journal Book of the Royal Society*, entry for 28 November 1660, quoted in *Encyclopaedia Britannica*, 1963 edn, vol. 19, p. 597, bottom first column entry on Royal Society.
3. Robert Hooke, *Micrographia or Physiological Descriptions of Minute bodies made by the help of Magnifying Glasses*, London, 1665, preface. Quoted in H. Hutchinson, *Sir Christopher Wren*, Gollancz, London, 1976, p. 33.
4. W. Ward, *Lives of the Professors of Gresham College*, London, 1740. Quoted in the *DNB*, p. 995, C. Wren.
5. Balthasar de Monconys, *Voyages d'Angleterre*, Paris, 1663, ed. M.C. Henry, Paris, 1887, pp. 61–76. Quoted in Hutchinson, p. 43, see above.

CHAPTER THREE

1. Roger Pratt, notebooks, quoted in R.T. Gunther, *The Architecture of Sir Roger Pratt*, Oxford University Press, Oxford, 1928. Quoted in J. Chambers, *The English House*, Methuen, London; Norton, New York, 1985, p. 88.

Notes

Chapter Four

1. Wren, *Parentalia*, ch. 2, n. 1, pl. 9. *Transactions of the Wren Society*, ed. A.T. Bolton and H.D. Hendry, OUP, Oxford, 1924–43, vol. XIX, pp. 152–3.
2. Robert Hooke, *Diary*, 1672–80, ed. H.W. Robinson and F. Adams, Taylor and Francis, London, 1935, entry for 1 September 1673.
3. Hooke, *Diary*, entry for 14 November 1679.

Chapter Five

1. Wren, *Parentalia*, ch. 2, n. 1, p. 283.
2. *The Diary of John Evelyn*, ch. 1, n. 1, entry for 2 December 1697. Quoted in Hutchinson, see ch. 2, n. 3 above.

Chapter Six

1. Letter to Dean Fell of Christ Church, Oxford, dated 3 December 1681, in *Transactions of the Wren Society*, ch. 4, n. 1, vol. V, p. 21.

BIBLIOGRAPHY

Andrade, E.N. da C. *A Brief History of the Royal Society*, The Royal Society, London, 1960

Beard, Geoffrey, and Kersting, Anthony. *The Work of Christopher Wren*, Bloomsbury, London, 1987

Bennett, J.A. *The Mathematical Science of Christopher Wren*, Cambridge University Press, Cambridge, 1982

Briggs, Martin. *Wren, the Incomparable*, George Allen & Unwin, London, 1953

De Maré, Eric. *Wren's London*, The Folio Society, London, 1975

Downes, Kerry. *English Baroque Architecture*, A. Zwemmer, London, 1966

——. *Hawksmoor*, Thames & Hudson, London 1969

——. *Christopher Wren*, Penguin, London, 1971

——. *Vanbrugh*, A. Zwemmer, London, 1977

Dutton, Ralph. *The Age of Wren*, Batsford, London, 1951

Espinasse, Margaret. *Robert Hooke*, Heinemann, London, 1956

Hutchinson, Harold. *Sir Christopher Wren*, Gollancz, London, 1976

Jeffrey, Paul. *The City Churches of Christopher Wren*, Hambledon, London, 1996

Loftie, William. *Inigo Jones and Wren or, The Rise and Decline of Modern Architecture in England*, Rivington, London, 1893

Bibliography

Sekler, Eduard. *Wren and his Place in European Architecture*, Faber & Faber, London, 1956

Summerson, Sir John. *Sir Christopher Wren*, Collins, London, 1953

Whinney, Margaret. *Wren*, Thames & Hudson, London, 1971

POCKET BIOGRAPHIES

AVAILABLE

Beethoven
Anne Pimlott Baker

Scott of the Antarctic
Michael De-la-Noy

Alexander the Great
E.E. Rice

Sigmund Freud
Stephen Wilson

Marilyn Monroe
Sheridan Morley and
Ruth Leon

Rasputin
Harold Shukman

Jane Austen
Helen Lefroy

Mao Zedong
Delia Davin

Marie and Pierre Curie
John Senior

Ellen Terry
Moira Shearer

POCKET BIOGRAPHIES

David Livingstone
C.S. Nicholls

Margot Fonteyn
Alastair Macaulay

Winston Churchill
Robert Blake

Abraham Lincoln
H.G. Pitt

Charles Dickens
Catherine Peters

Enid Blyton
George Greenfield

George IV
Michael De-la-Noy

Christopher Wren
James Chambers

Che Guevara
Andrew Sinclair

POCKET BIOGRAPHIES

FORTHCOMING

W.G. Grace
Donald Trelford

The Brontës
Kathryn White

Lawrence of Arabia
Jeremy Wilson

Christopher Columbus
Peter Rivière

Martin Luther King
Harry Harmer

For a copy of our complete list or details of other Sutton titles, please contact Regina Schinner at Sutton Publishing Limited, Phoenix Mill, Thrupp, Stroud, Gloucestershire, GL5 2BU